S. Hrg. 113–458

EVALUATING U.S. POLICY ON TAIWAN ON THE 35TH ANNIVERSARY OF THE TAIWAN RELATIONS ACT (TRA)

HEARING

BEFORE THE

SUBCOMMITTEE ON EAST ASIAN AND PACIFIC AFFAIRS

OF THE

COMMITTEE ON FOREIGN RELATIONS UNITED STATES SENATE

ONE HUNDRED THIRTEENTH CONGRESS

SECOND SESSION

APRIL 3, 2014

Printed for the use of the Committee on Foreign Relations

Available via the World Wide Web: http://www.gpo.gov/fdsys/

U.S. GOVERNMENT PRINTING OFFICE

91–138 PDF   WASHINGTON : 2014

For sale by the Superintendent of Documents, U.S. Government Printing Office
Internet: bookstore.gpo.gov   Phone: toll free (866) 512–1800; DC area (202) 512–1800
Fax: (202) 512–2104   Mail: Stop IDCC, Washington, DC 20402–0001

COMMITTEE ON FOREIGN RELATIONS

ROBERT MENENDEZ, New Jersey, *Chairman*

BARBARA BOXER, California
BENJAMIN L. CARDIN, Maryland
JEANNE SHAHEEN, New Hampshire
CHRISTOPHER A. COONS, Delaware
RICHARD J. DURBIN, Illinois
TOM UDALL, New Mexico
CHRISTOPHER MURPHY, Connecticut
TIM KAINE, Virginia
EDWARD J. MARKEY, Massachusetts

BOB CORKER, Tennessee
JAMES E. RISCH, Idaho
MARCO RUBIO, Florida
RON JOHNSON, Wisconsin
JEFF FLAKE, Arizona
JOHN McCAIN, Arizona
JOHN BARRASSO, Wyoming
RAND PAUL, Kentucky

DANIEL E. O'BRIEN, *Staff Director*
LESTER E. MUNSON III, *Republican Staff Director*

———————

SUBCOMMITTEE ON EAST ASIAN AND PACIFIC AFFAIRS

BENJAMIN L. CARDIN, Maryland, *Chairman*

CHRISTOPHER MURPHY, Connecticut
BARBARA BOXER, California
TOM UDALL, New Mexico
EDWARD J. MARKEY, Massachusetts

MARCO RUBIO, Florida
RON JOHNSON, Wisconsin
JEFF FLAKE, Arizona
JOHN McCAIN, Arizona

(II)

CONTENTS

(III)

EVALUATING U.S. POLICY ON TAIWAN ON THE 35TH ANNIVERSARY OF THE TAIWAN RELATIONS ACT (TRA)

THURSDAY, APRIL 3, 2014

U.S. SENATE,
SUBCOMMITTEE ON EAST ASIAN AND PACIFIC AFFAIRS,
COMMITTEE ON FOREIGN RELATIONS,
Washington, DC.

The subcommittee met, pursuant to notice, at 10:01 a.m., in room SD–419, Dirksen Senate Office Building, Hon. Benjamin L. Cardin (chairman of the subcommittee) presiding.

Present: Senators Cardin, Murphy, and Rubio.

OPENING STATEMENT OF HON. BENJAMIN L. CARDIN, U.S. SENATOR FROM MARYLAND

Senator CARDIN. Well, good morning, and welcome to the Subcommittee on East Asian and Pacific Affairs.

Our hearing today will be to evaluating the U.S. policy on Taiwan on the 35th anniversary of the Taiwan Relations Act.

Let me say from the outset I know that Senator Rubio will be joining me shortly. He indicated he may be a few minutes late getting here. I know Senator Murphy will also be joining me. There is a great deal of interest, I can assure you, in the United States Senate and on the Senate Foreign Relations Committee on United States-Taiwan relations. It has been some time since we have held a hearing. I think it was 1999, the last hearing that we held on Taiwan. So this is a particularly important hearing.

I say from the beginning on an apologetic note this is a pretty busy time in the United States Senate. As this committee is meeting, two other committees that I serve on are holding markups on legislation, including the Senate Finance Committee and Environment and Public Works Committee. So for the sake of the people of Maryland who I represent, I am going to have to dodge out of here during the hearing to offer certain amendments that are important to not only Marylanders but to our country. So I apologize to the witnesses that I will not be here for the entire hearing, but I can assure you that the importance of this hearing is top on our agenda.

And I thank all of our witnesses for being here and for their participation in this hearing.

Last month, the subcommittee held a hearing on our alliances in Northeast Asia. So today we will be evaluating another important

2

part of our Rebalance to Asia, the relationship that we have with Taiwan.

On April 10, 1979, Congress enacted the Taiwan Relations Act, a bill designed to help maintain peace, security, and stability in the western Pacific and to promote the foreign policy of the United States by authorizing the continuation of commercial, cultural, and other relations between the people of the United States and the people of Taiwan. The act also led to the establishment of the American Institute of Taipei. Thirty-five years later, the framework provided by this legislation continues to govern U.S. policy in the region.

Taiwan has been and remains one of our most important partners in Asia. Taiwan has a vibrant democracy, shares common values with the United States, boasts an advanced economy, and serves as a strong security partner and leader in the region.

Within this context of shared values, let me just note that within our thriving democracy, there will be disagreements and there will be differences of opinion among people, as we have seen recently in Taiwan. Democracies allow for this kind of vigorous political dialogue. Through constructive and peaceful discussions with all sides, these differences can be resolved.

Taiwan is the 12th-largest U.S. trading partner. Thousands of people visit the United States from Taiwan each year, contributing over $1.2 billion to the U.S. economy in 2012. And on a personal note, let me say the relationship between the people of Maryland and the people of Taiwan has been very strong. The commerce that goes through the Port of Baltimore from Taiwan is very important to the economy of our region.

And President Ma has demonstrated leadership and creativity in handling and resolving disputes with Taiwan's neighbors, particularly with the historical agreement in 2012 between Japan and Taiwan over the fishery resources near the Senkaku Islands. This agreement serves as an important model for the region and indicates the important role Taiwan can and should play on the international stage.

My colleagues in both the Senate and House have supported a role for Taiwan within the international stage. I was pleased to cosponsor legislation introduced last year in the Senate to further this goal by directing the Department of State to develop a strategy to obtain observer status for Taiwan in the International Civil Aviation Organization. I hope we see positive progress in this area.

We also see a growing and positive relationship between Taiwan and the People's Republic of China over the last 6 years. Taiwan and the PRC have signed 21 economic or functional agreements, including the Economic Cooperation Framework Agreement. In February, officials from Taiwan and PRC in charge of cross-strait affairs held their first formal meeting since 1949, opening the doors for further communication. There is progress being made for security in that region. The United States has long welcomed steps such as these to improve relationships and reduce tensions. And we certainly hope cross-strait relations progress will continue on a positive trajectory.

Although relations have improved, we continue to see an expansion of the People's Republic of China's military capabilities, which are often aimed at Taiwan. This is troubling. In this context, the United States-Taiwan security relationship must remain a priority.

The challenges and opportunities in the region have changed since 1979. Nevertheless, the TRA continues to provide a solid foundation to guide our policy.

The United States has an interest in maintaining a peaceful, prosperous, and secure East Asia, and recognizing this, the Obama administration has made a commitment to rebalance toward Asia. The United States relationship with Taiwan is a critical piece in this strategy, and as such, it is important for the United States Government, both the executive and legislative branches, to regularly reaffirm our enduring commitment to Taiwan.

As I mentioned earlier, the last time this committee held a hearing on the Taiwan Relations Act was 1999. Today provides an important opportunity to assure our partners that the United States remains committed to this important relationship.

So I look forward to hearing from both of our panels today as to how the current state of affairs are between Taiwan and the United States and how that fits into the Rebalance to Asia and security and prosperity within that region.

We have been joined by Senator Murphy, and as I explained earlier, Senator Murphy will take the gavel a little bit later on in this hearing. And I thank him for being here and would yield if he would like to make some opening comments.

Senator MURPHY. I look forward to hearing from the witnesses.

Senator CARDIN. Thank you.

On our first panel, we are pleased to have Mr. Daniel Russel. He is no stranger to this committee. He has appeared before our committee on several occasions. The Assistant Secretary of State for the Bureau of East Asian and Pacific Affairs at the Department of State, Mr. Russel, began his tour as Assistant Secretary on July 13, 2013. He previously served at the White House as Special Assistant to the President and National Security Staff Senior Director for Asian Affairs.

I know that Secretary Russel is going to be very busy with the President's planned trip to Asia coming up shortly. I know that he will be very busy planning to make sure that visit is as productive as possible in terms of our Rebalance to Asia.

Secretary Russel, it is a pleasure to have you.

As is the custom of this committee, all the witnesses' full statements will be made part of the record, and you may proceed as you wish.

STATEMENT OF DANIEL R. RUSSEL, ASSISTANT SECRETARY FOR EAST ASIAN AND PACIFIC AFFAIRS, U.S. DEPARTMENT OF STATE, WASHINGTON, DC

Mr. RUSSEL. Thank you very much, Mr. Chairman and Senator Murphy, for this opportunity to testify on United States-Taiwan relations.

The United States relationship with Taiwan is based on the three joint communiques and the Taiwan Relations Act, the TRA, which as you noted was signed into law 35 years ago next week.

The framework that Congress established in the TRA has fostered the development and resilience of our relations with Taiwan over the past 35 years. The United States-Taiwan relationship is grounded in history and shared values and our common commitment to democracy and human rights. Taiwan and the TRA enjoyed genuine bipartisan support. The Taiwan Caucus in the Senate and House contains one-fourth of sitting Senators and Representatives, divided about equally by party. And I think that is important.

I am here to report that the United States-Taiwan unofficial relations have never been better. Let me give you four reasons why.

First, we share prosperity. Taiwan is now our 12th-largest trading partner and has invested almost $8 billion in the United States. That creates jobs here.

Second, we learn from each other. Taiwan is the sixth-largest sender of students to the United States.

Third, we each have an interest in promoting and improving cross-strait relations. The enduring United States support for Taiwan and for its self-defense helps give Taiwan the confidence to strengthen its relations with the PRC which, in turn, supports regional peace and stability.

Fourth, we work together. We work together in the international community. For example, Taiwan's quick assistance to the Philippines after Typhoon Haiyan complemented United States relief efforts there.

Taiwan is one of the world's largest economies. Taiwan is a focus market under the Commerce Department's SelectUSA program to promote investment in the United States. Consultations tomorrow under our Trade and Investment Framework Agreement, TIFA talks, offer the prospect of important progress supporting United States stakeholders, supporting President Ma's own economic reforms, and importantly, supporting the diversification of Taiwan's economy.

Congress created the American Institute in Taiwan, AIT, in part to advance these economic ties, as well as cultural ties, and this strategy has worked. Taiwan now sends more students to the United States than Japan or than Mexico.

Taiwan also participates in about 60 international organizations, as well as hundreds of international nongovernment organizations. The United States supports Taiwan's membership in international organizations that do not require statehood for membership and meaningful participation in others. Congress, with strong bipartisan and bicameral votes, support Taiwan's participation in the triennial International Civil Aviation Organization, the ICAO, assembly last year in the resolution that you cosponsored. We welcome Taiwan's participation and we support Taiwan's expanded participation in the future.

We also encourage the United Nations, its agencies, and other international organizations to increase Taiwan's participation in technical or expert meetings.

And as I said, Taiwan's role as a responsible global player is shown by its disaster relief efforts. Taiwan was quick to contribute to the initial search in the South China Sea for Malaysian Airlines 370 and quickly provided assistance to other nations following Typhoon Haiyan. Simply put, Taiwan is a reliable partner and a capable friend who contributes to regional peace and security.

Mr. Chairman, the maintenance of peace across the Taiwan Strait is crucial to stability and prosperity throughout the Asia-Pacific. The Obama administration has notified over 12 billion dollars' worth of arms sales to Taiwan, a testament to how seriously we take our obligation to assist Taiwan in maintaining a sufficient self-defense force.

Beyond arms sales, the United States engages in a wide range of important security consultations and exchanges in order to assist Taiwan Armed Forces as they maintain, train, and equip themselves.

I am convinced, as I said, that strong United States support for Taiwan helps give our friends the confidence to strengthen cross-strait relations. We welcome those improved relations in trade, travel, science, and other forms of cooperation unimaginable a decade ago. They benefit both sides. They benefit regional security. They benefit the United States relationship with China, and they benefit our unofficial relations with Taiwan.

And to reiterate our long-held position, resolution of differences across the strait must be peaceful and without coercion in accordance with the wishes of the people on both sides.

So thank you for allowing me to help mark the 35th anniversary of the TRA. The United States sees a future of increased cooperation and flourishing unofficial relations between the people of the United States and the people of Taiwan.

Thank you.

[The prepared statement of Mr. Russel follows:]

PREPARED STATEMENT OF DANIEL R. RUSSEL

INTRODUCTION

Thank you for inviting me to this special subcommittee meeting on Taiwan. Next week is the 35th anniversary of the Taiwan Relations Act (TRA). I wish to commend you, Mr. Chairman, for your leadership and many years of strong interest on behalf of U.S.-Taiwan relations and their role in regional prosperity and stability.

The unofficial U.S.-Taiwan relationship has never been stronger than it is today, and it underscores our firm commitment to the Taiwan Relations Act. Strengthening our relations with Taiwan and our longstanding friendship with the people on Taiwan remains a key element of the U.S. strategic rebalance to the Asia-Pacific. U.S.-Taiwan relations are grounded in history, respect for democracy and human rights, respect for international rules and norms, a growing economic partnership, and enduring security cooperation.

Taiwan's status today as a top-20 world economy is a testimony to the diligence of the people on Taiwan and to the success of the TRA. It is a leading player in regional development, conservation, and assistance efforts—as it confidently engages the People's Republic of China.

The United States has an abiding interest in peace and stability across the strait. Toward that end, the United States supports and encourages improvements in cross-strait relations, albeit at a pace acceptable to the people on both sides. Strong United States support for Taiwan autonomy also helps give our friends in Taiwan the confidence to strengthen their cross-strait relations, as we have seen in recent years. At the same time, we support Taiwan's effort to participate in the international community in a manner befitting a large economy and modern society with a great deal to contribute.

ECONOMIC AND CULTURAL TIES

The United States substantive and robust unofficial relations with Taiwan have developed markedly under the framework of the TRA over the past 35 years, allowing us to cooperate in a wide range of mutually beneficial areas including energy, the environment, and scientific research, to name a few. Over the past 35 years, Taiwan has grown to be one of the world's largest economies; today Taiwan is our

12th-largest trading partner and a top-10 destination for U.S. agricultural and food exports. There also is significant two-way direct investment that spurs growth in both of our economies, with over $16 billion of direct investment positions by U.S. firms in Taiwan in 2012 and close to $8 billion of foreign direct investment from Taiwan in the United States during the same period.

Taiwan was the sixth-largest source of international students in the United States through the 2012–2013 academic year. On a proportional basis, Taiwan sends more students to the United States than even mainland China or India. In terms of absolute numbers, Taiwan sends more students to the United States than Japan, Mexico, Turkey, Brazil, or the U.K. do.

The Visa Waiver Program (VWP), to which Taiwan was admitted in November 2012, has led to increased tourist and business travel from Taiwan. Foreign visitors to the United States generate stateside jobs, and we are pleased that in the 8 months after Taiwan joined the VWP Taiwan travel to the United States increased more than 29 percent.

We work cooperatively with Taiwan on many issues of importance to the region and the international community, to include WHO efforts on pandemic prevention, detection and treatment; APEC and WTO efforts to expand trade and investment opportunities; and U.N. and NGO efforts to promote responsible civil aviation and environmental protection.

We have a very busy and active agenda with Taiwan to discuss substantive areas of cooperation and mutual interests. For example, just recently:

- A Commerce Department Deputy Assistant Secretary participated in an APEC Working Group meeting hosted by Taiwan and then worked with the American Institute in Taiwan (AIT) to promote U.S. exports to Taiwan and encourage more business investment in the United States from Taiwan. Taiwan has been identified as a focus market under the SelectUSA program to promote and facilitate foreign direct investment to the United States. A single Taiwan company is now engaged in a $2 billion expansion of its petrochemical facilities in the United States, and promotion of the United States as an investment destination could generate several billion more dollars in Taiwan investment in the coming years.
- One of my State Department colleagues participated in a regional meeting of Fulbright Executive Directors, hosted in Taiwan this year, to promote scholarly exchanges, international education, and people-to-people outreach. Taiwan's mature Fulbright program serves as a model of cultural exchange to the region and the world.
- And another State Department colleague met with AIT and Taiwan authorities to discuss Taiwan's meaningful participation in international organizations and Taiwan's ability to contribute to humanitarian assistance and disaster relief efforts in the region. We were pleased in September 2013 to see Taiwan invited to participate in the General Assembly of the International Civil Aviation Organization (ICAO), and we would like to build on that success in a variety of organizations.

We are also very active on the economic and commercial front. In March 2013, we resumed our engagement with Taiwan under our Trade and Investment Framework Agreement (TIFA). Through the TIFA we are addressing a number of U.S. and Taiwan trade and investment concerns, including in the areas of agriculture, intellectual property rights (IPR), investment, pharmaceuticals and medical devices, and technical barriers to trade. We have made progress in this forum since its resumption last year and look forward to a productive TIFA meeting on April 4. We look forward to learning more about Taiwan's economic reforms spurred by President Ma's New Year Address.

The Department of Commerce leads the SelectUSA program that promotes business investment in the United States. For our part, we encourage U.S. State and local governments to include Taiwan among the destinations for their business development missions. Among the factors that are luring corporate leaders in Taiwan to take a close look at the United States as a manufacturing hub or as an export platform are the strong rule of law and protection for intellectual property rights that we enjoy in the United States; the research and development capabilities of U.S. companies, universities, and laboratories; and the price and supply of natural gas in the United States.

In October 2013, Taiwan sent one of the largest delegations to the SelectUSA summit organized by the Department of Commerce. In November, Taiwan's former Vice President, Vincent Siew, led an impressive delegation of Taiwan CEOs to the United States, with over $2 billion of new or ongoing investments in the United

States announced during the visit. We are now looking at how to regularize these kinds of business exchanges.

The United States remains by far the largest investor in Asia, as well as on Taiwan. The number of registered Americans living on Taiwan increased 2.7 percent in 2013 to 67,510 people. The United States remains one of Taiwan travelers' most popular tourist destinations.

In 2013 the United States and Taiwan celebrated 20 years of environmental cooperation, during which time Taiwan made huge strides in reducing pollution and becoming a regional leader in environmental best practices. We are working with Taiwan authorities to identify productive ways for them to share their experiences and lessons learned in this field with countries in the region and beyond.

In addition, we enjoy ongoing and robust exchanges with Taiwan defense and military service leadership personnel.

SECURITY TIES

Consistent with the Taiwan Relations Act and the United States one China policy including the three communiques, the United States makes available to Taiwan defense articles and defense services in such quantity as may be necessary to enable Taiwan to maintain a sufficient self-defense capability. This longstanding policy contributes to the maintenance of peace and stability across the Taiwan Strait.

The TRA states that peace and stability in the Western Pacific area "are in the political, security, and economic interests of the United States, and are matters of international concern." This is as true today as it was in 1979, if not more so. It also asserts a U.S. policy to "maintain the capacity of the United States to resist any resort to force or other forms of coercion that would jeopardize the security, or the social or economic system, of the people on Taiwan." The United States is firmly committed to this policy.

As China's economy and military spending grow, and China continues to carry out military deployments and exercises aimed at Taiwan, it is more important than ever for Taiwan to invest sufficiently in a professional military force that uses asymmetry, innovation, and other defensive advantages to deter potential attempts at coercion or aggression. For its part, the Obama administration has notified to Congress over $12 billion of sales of defensive equipment and materials to Taiwan. This is a tangible sign of our determination to assist Taiwan in maintaining a sufficient self-defense.

Our security relations with Taiwan are about much more than arms sales. The United States engages in a wide range of consultations and exchanges with Taiwan in order to assist Taiwan Armed Forces as they seek to maintain, train, and equip a capable, effective self-defense capability.

Taiwan does not formally participate in international coalitions or exercises. However, Taiwan uses defensive materials and services provided by the United States to enhance its humanitarian assistance capacity. Taiwan plays an increasingly significant role in disaster relief, such as after the 2008 Sichuan earthquake; after the 2011 earthquake and tsunami in Japan; after Typhoon Haiyan in November 2013 in the Philippines and in Palau; and immediately after the disappearance last month of Malaysia Air 370 when international participants were focusing on searching the South China Sea.

Our support for Taiwan's security and its defensive needs has given Taipei confidence in its engagements with Beijing, leading Taiwan to sign an unprecedented number of economic and cultural cross-strait agreements. Soon there will be more than 800 direct flights a week between Taiwan and the mainland, something unthinkable a decade ago. Taiwan's Mainland Affairs Office Director Wang Yu-chi recently traveled to the mainland for meetings with his PRC counterpart, Director Zhang Zhijun of the PRC's Taiwan Affairs Office. The United States continues to support these and other cross-strait dialogues at a pace acceptable to people on both sides of the strait, and remains committed to supporting Taiwan's ability to engage in such discourse free from coercion.

The United States welcomes Taiwan's efforts to resolve disputes peacefully, approach territorial and maritime disputes pragmatically, and share resources in these disputed areas. For example, in 2013 Taiwan reached a fisheries agreement with Japan that allows both sides to fish in the East China Sea, and also resolved a fisheries incident with the Philippines through consultation. These examples serve as a model for the region of Taiwan's ability to peacefully resolve maritime issues through diplomatic means.

INTERNATIONAL SPACE FOR TAIWAN

As a top-20 world economy and a WTO and APEC member, Taiwan has a strong role to play in the Asia-Pacific region and worldwide. Taiwan participates in about 60 international organizations as well as hundreds of international NGOs.

We are pleased that since 2009 Taiwan has been invited each year to participate in the World Health Assembly (WHA) as an observer, and we expect Taiwan to participate in next month's WHA as well. We think Taiwan's status at the WHA also should allow for more meaningful participation in the work of the World Health Organization, through greater inclusion in technical and expert meetings, including those related to the Pandemic Influenza Preparedness Framework (PIP) and the International Food Safety Authorities Network (INFOSAN). In September 2013, Taiwan was invited as a guest to the triennial ICAO Assembly in Montreal, and we look forward to Taiwan's expanded participation in ICAO. Through a Taiwan NGO, Taiwan also observes and participates in the United Nations (U.N.) Framework Convention on Climate Change.

The United States supports Taiwan's membership in international organizations where statehood is not a requirement for membership, and we encourage Taiwan's meaningful participation in other organizations. U.S. goals for supporting Taiwan's participation include: enabling the people on Taiwan to comply with international regulations and safety, addressing transborder health issues, facilitating international travel, giving and receiving appropriate international assistance and advice, and assisting in capacity-building.

Consistent with this longstanding policy, the State Department encourages the U.N., its agencies, and other international organizations to increase Taiwan's meaningful participation in technical and expert meetings. Taiwan has the resources and expertise to play a constructive role in the work of those agencies.

CONCLUSION

AIT and many U.S. departments and agencies have meaningful, substantive engagements with Taiwan as part of our strong commercial, cultural and other relations. Looking forward, we see increased opportunities for cooperation on issues concerning trade, health, cultural exchanges, and security, and we remain committed to seizing them.

Mr. Chairman and members of the committee, I thank you again for the opportunity to appear today to highlight the strength and durability of ties between the people of the United States and the people on Taiwan. Taiwan has earned a respected place in the world. Thanks to the Taiwan Relations Act, over the past 35 years, the United States and Taiwan have enjoyed a firm foundation of friendship that we continue to build today.

Senator CARDIN. Well, again, Secretary Russel, thank you for your service. Thank you for your testimony.

The language that you used in regards to the cross-strait issues is very similar to the maritime security issues. We want these issues resolved, direct discussions among the parties involved, peacefully with respect for the rights of all the people in the region. So I could not agree with you more.

I mentioned in my opening statement the agreement reached between Taiwan and Japan in regards to fishing rights. Can we learn something from the way that Taiwan and Japan handled that particular issue that could be helpful in dealing not just with the cross-strait issues but dealing with maritime security problems in that region?

Mr. RUSSEL. Yes. Thank you, Mr. Chairman. I agree with you that that agreement between Japan and Taiwan on fisheries in the East China Sea is very important. We see it, frankly, as a model for the peaceful resolution through diplomatic means of practical problems relating to resources that derive from underlying disputes over maritime claims.

The existence of territorial claims does not, and should not, preclude the ability of claimants to make common cause to find peaceful and effective ways to work together and particularly to responsibly share and manage the resources in the waters of the South China Sea or the East China Sea, whether we are talking about marine life and fishing or whether we are talking about undersea hydrocarbon, oil and gas.

This principle, which was also enunciated in President Ma's own East Asia Peace and Cooperation Initiative—this principle of peaceful resolution is germane to all of the disputes, and it is incumbent on all of the claimants to foreswear intimidation, coercion, and other nondiplomatic or extra-legal means.

Senator CARDIN. Help me understand how we are going to reconcile the Trans-Pacific Partnership, TPP, and our economic relations with Taiwan and Taiwan's economic relations in the region. We all hope that we will be able to reconcile 10 countries in the Pacific on an agreement. We are including many of our major trading partners in the TPP agreement. Taiwan has a robust economic relationship with the United States. And I think Taiwan has expressed interest in what is going on, as far as the TPP is concerned.

What is the administration's position as it relates to TPP and our economic ties with Taiwan and Taiwan's ties with the Pacific?

Mr. RUSSEL. Well, thank you, Mr. Chairman.

Our long-term priority throughout the entire Asia-Pacific region is to help create an environment that is genuinely open to U.S. exports of goods and services. We stand for free trade, and we are working for free trade.

In particular, my good friend and colleague, Ambassador Mike Froman, and my other colleagues at the U.S. Trade Representative are hard at work with 11 of our partners in the TPP process in an effort to conclude the current round.

Now, the first job at hand for us is to successfully conclude TPP among the existing 12 members, but it is true, as you point out, Mr. Chairman, that Taiwan is an extremely important economy in the region and is an important trading partner for the United States. And on that basis, we have indicated that we welcome Taiwan's interest in the TPP.

Now, as a practical matter, tomorrow, as I mentioned in my testimony, the same colleagues at the U.S. Trade Representative's office will be meeting with Taiwan representatives under the TIFA talks, the Trade and Investment Framework Agreement. I think it is very important that these talks have restarted, that this effort is underway. Our principal focus is and should be on addressing the outstanding issues between the United States and Taiwan through this framework. We can, by doing so, build momentum for expanding our trade and investment regimes and demonstrating Taiwan's own ability to take necessary reform measures on the trade front.

I would add, if I may, that the United States and Taiwan have made great strides also in terms of investment and that the active, robust, and effective participation of an impressive delegation from Taiwan in the SelectUSA forum, hosted by President Obama with Secretary Kerry and Secretary Pritzker late last year, opened the door to a hoped-for increase in Taiwan investment in the United States.

Senator CARDIN. We talked about the fact that we want matters resolved peacefully. We have talked about the fact that we want people sitting at the table resolving issues. So Taiwan needs to have a seat at the table in international discussions. We have strongly supported their ability to participate in aviation.

How do you see the ability of Taiwan to have a meaningful role on the international stage to be able to protect the rights of the people that live in Taiwan, as well as the regional security, economic, and safety issues?

Mr. RUSSEL. Well, thank you, Mr. Chairman.

We are convinced that Taiwan has a great deal to contribute to the international community. Taiwan has tremendous resources. It has tremendous experience and tremendous expertise. The world needs Taiwan's help in addressing a plethora of global challenges and issues, and consistent with the legislation that you cosponsored, but more importantly as a function of fundamental United States policy, we have and continue strongly to support Taiwan's active participation in international organizations for which statehood is not a requirement, but active and meaningful roles in other organizations as well. And we partner closely with Taiwan in a number of areas.

In terms of organizations, as you know, Taiwan and we were successful in enabling its participation in the ICAO meetings late last year, and that is an area where we will continue to work. There are other organizations as well where we strongly advocate for an appropriate role for Taiwan.

We think that increasing Taiwan's international space also affords its people dignity and helps provide it with the confidence it needs to engage China in cross-straits relations. And we make the case to the Chinese, Mr. Chairman, that it is in China's interest as well from our perspective to enable Taiwan appropriately to contribute.

Senator CARDIN. Thank you.

Senator Rubio.

Senator RUBIO. Thank you, Mr. Chairman.

Thank you for being with us today. We appreciate it very much.

We have read a lot and heard a lot about this rebalance toward Asia and we have seen some actions in that regard. Of course, we are reevaluating our defense relationship with Japan and seeing how we can increase cooperation. They have got some internal constitutional issues they have to work through, but we have seen that. We have certainly seen a reinvigoration or a re-upping of our situation with South Korea and, of course, have a free trade agreement with them. And even with the Philippines, there is now talk about creating a rotational presence in terms of the United States being involved. We know they have now gone to arbitration on their claims with regard to China. So we have seen activity there.

Tell us a little bit. What is the role of Taiwan in the United States rebalance or pivot toward Asia?

Mr. RUSSEL. Thank you very much, Senator, for all of your work on these issues and for your thoughtful question.

The Obama administration has placed a high priority on strengthening our own official relations with Taiwan as part of our overall rebalance to the Asia-Pacific region in part because Taiwan

11

shares our values and our commitment to democracy, in part because of the important history and ties that bind us, but also in part because of the dynamism and potential of the Taiwan economy. And therefore, our security cooperation, our economic cooperation, our people-to-people and other forms of cooperation, including multinational cooperation, has continued to grow and we see further room to grow.

One outstanding example has been the role that Taiwan played in assisting in the relief efforts in response to Super Typhoon Haiyan in the Philippines. Another is the readiness with which Taiwan responded to the loss of Malaysian Air Flight 370 and actively contributed initially to the search and rescue efforts.

We have reached an agreement last year on a visa waiver program, a status for Taiwan that has opened the door to tourism and the people-to-people exchange that will deepen ties and benefit the United States, including through educational exchange. The TIFA talks that begin again in Washington tomorrow help us strengthen and expand our economic relationship, and the former Vice President of Taiwan, Vincent Siew, late last year led an extraordinary delegation of top CEOs interested in finding ways to expand investment in the United States. So I think that the economic connection between the United States and Taiwan relates directly to the economic underpinnings of our rebalance.

Senator RUBIO. Because I do not want to run out of time, let me ask you in specific because in the world everything is interrelated. I would venture to guess and, in fact, I am pretty sure of the fact that Taiwan has watched with great interest what has happened with Crimea where both the economic leverage that Russia has on Europe as a whole and in particular on Ukraine and, of course, its military abilities in comparison to the Ukraine allowed Russia to basically invade and take a piece of land away from a neighbor and annex it and basically occupy it as they do today. And I would venture to guess that the similarities for the Taiwanese is pretty striking to the fact that in—for example, even as late as last year, our own defense analysis found that the primary purpose behind the military investment by China is to prepare for a conflict in the Taiwan Strait.

So what are we doing in that regard to ensure that that calculation does not change to the point where China believes they can move aggressively on retaking Taiwan without having any sort of consequence for it, in essence, their belief that they could pretty much replicate what Russia did to Crimea? What steps have we taken to ensure that that does not happen, that that balance is not unsettled to the point where you are actually inviting China to do something like that?

Mr. RUSSEL. Thank you, Senator.

First and foremost, the key underpinning of our policy rooted in TRA is our opposition to any effort to resolve the differences pertaining to Taiwan through intimidation, through coercion, or through military force. And maintenance of peace and stability in the cross-strait is a top priority.

That is why the Obama administration, long before the crisis in Crimea at the beginning of the President's first term, has taken such robust steps to enable Taiwan to maintain a sufficient self-

12

defense capability by providing arms of a defensive character. The Obama administration has notified over $12 billion in arms sales to Taiwan already. And at least as important, the United States has intensified our dialogue and consultations with Taiwan on defense issues and on defense strategy.

We similarly have a robust dialogue with China. Now, we do not, as a matter of policy, ever discuss or consult in advance with China regarding weapons sales to Taiwan or possible sales, but we do discuss the situation in the strait regularly with China and make very clear to them our commitment not only to our One China Policy and the three United States-China joint communiques but also to the Taiwan Relations Act.

Senator RUBIO. I do not know if we are going to do a second round since there are not that many folks here. But let me just ask you this, again, because the world is interrelated. If, in fact, the United States reaches an agreement with Iran that allows Iran to enrich uranium and reprocess plutonium, at that point how would we go to Taiwan and say you should never do this, however? We allow our enemies and our adversaries to enrich and to reprocess, but our friends like you who are similarly threatened or feel threatened, I should say, are not allowed to provide—how do we go to Taiwan or Korea or Japan for that matter and argue to them that they should continue to walk away from a nuclear weapons capability or an enrichment capability when we are basically—if, in fact, we acquiesce to other countries with hostile intentions having that sort of capability?

Mr. RUSSEL. Senator, I do not accept the premise that the security of either Taiwan or Japan or Korea would be enhanced by an advancement or transformation of their peaceful civil nuclear programs into a nuclear weapons program, and I see no evidence that the leaders in Taiwan or Japan or Korea are of that view either.

In the case of Taiwan, as I said, we have an extensive ongoing set of consultations regarding Taiwan's legitimate self-defense needs. It begins with the software. It begins with the strategy, and we have significantly advanced our discussions about the steps that Taiwan can and should take with regard to recruitment, retention, doctrine, asymmetric warfare capabilities, and decisions about necessary weapons flow from that strategy.

More broadly, I think that the lesson that our allies, Japan and Korea, derive from the Iran experience is that strong unity and resolve can compel an unwilling nation to make the decision to pursue serious negotiations as the way out. And this very much informs our approach and our strategy to North Korea which is perhaps the——

Senator RUBIO. By the way, I do not dispute that the current leadership in South Korea and Japan and Taiwan do not want to pursue a weapons program, but I think that is largely built on the security assurances that the United States has historically made to all three of those countries over time. And I would just say that if, over time, those assurances erode either because our own capabilities are eroded through budget cuts and other means or because they come to question how committed the United States is to actually following through on these sorts of things, I think that people's calculations could change.

And that is a concern that I have about the region as a whole. I mean, there is a reason why both India and Pakistan now have nuclear weapons. There are multiple examples around the world where countries decide that they must provide for their own security.

And I point to the situation in Crimea simply because the Ukraine possessed the world's third-largest nuclear weapons stockpile at the end of the cold war and decided to walk away from that on assurances from the United Kingdom, the United States, and Russia that that coalition would provide for their security. As it turns out, one of the three countries that was supposed to provide for their security ended up invading them.

So I do think that over time this could have an impact on the thinking of leaders, and I just think that is important for us to keep in mind as we discuss why it is so important for the United States to have a robust commitment and capability to provide mutual defense of our allies in the region—Taiwan, Korea, and Japan. And that was the point I was trying to get to. If, in fact, that is ever eroded, in combination with any sort of agreement that allows hostile countries to enrich or reprocess, it could lead countries to conclude in the future that perhaps they are on their own, and if they are on their own, then they may need to pursue these sorts of, what they would view, insurance policies.

Mr. RUSSEL. Senator Rubio, I think you are making an extraordinarily important point, and I could not agree more that the credibility and the sustainability of the U.S. commitment that the Asia-Pacific is a strategic priority and that our presence, including as a security guarantor, is not in question is a paramount objective for U.S. foreign policy and for the Obama administration.

That conviction underlies the President's decision to travel later this month to Japan, to Korea, to Malaysia, to the Philippines, three treaty allies and a close friend and security partner of the United States. We are determined for the reasons that you stated and simply for the longer term U.S. interest to demonstrate our resolve and the robustness of our active engagement and participation both as a security partner and as an economic partner.

Senator RUBIO. I have one more question.

Senator MURPHY [presiding]. Yes, sure. Go ahead.

Senator RUBIO. Here is my last question. It is not an unreasonable hypothetical. This could have an impact on the whole region, but this is a region you oversee in general.

So as you are aware, the Philippines is currently involved in a dispute with China over some territory, and as a result, they have taken that case to arbitration before a panel that I believe will rule in their favor, or they are hopeful, will. The Chinese, of course, have made very strong threats against that and what that could mean.

Do you believe it is possible that at any time in the near future we could see China by force take these territories that they are disputing now with the Philippines? And if so, if they did so, what do you think the United States response would be and how would that be viewed by Taiwan and others in the region in particular? What impact would that have?

In fact, let me ask it this way. If, in fact, China basically just by force took Scarborough away from the Philippines and nothing happened, there was no impact of it? As I have heard some say, we are not going to go to war over some rocks. How would that impact the thinking in Taiwan and in other nations in the region with regard to the United States security commitment?

Mr. RUSSEL. Well, Senator, as your question implies, there is no doubt but that the United States allies in the region watch carefully how we are dealing with China in areas of potential dispute, the Taiwan Straits being one, the East China Sea and the South China Sea being others.

Right now, the South China Sea and the East China Sea have heated up, and there is a particular focus by the Chinese who are deploying large numbers of Coast Guard vessels to the area of the Second Thomas Shoal where the Philippines since 1999 maintained an outpost and conducting problematic behavior, including efforts to interfere with and interdict the routine resupply of the small garrison at the outpost.

Without treading on the treacherous ground of answering a hypothetical question per se, let me tell you this. I know that the President of the United States and the Obama administration is firmly committed to honoring our defense commitments to our allies. There should be no doubt about the resolve of the United States. We stand by our allies and we stand by our commitments.

That said, there is no reason why the issues pertaining to the South China Sea cannot be resolved through peaceful means. Diplomacy is the preferred vehicle, and when diplomacy does not yield results, states parties to the U.N. Convention on the Law of the Sea have the legitimate right to access the existing international legal mechanisms. That access, the filing of a claim under the tribunal at UNCLOS, occurred last weekend and is perhaps the proximate reason why the Chinese are expressing their anger and discontent on the sea through what to us appears to be intimidating steps.

The President of the United States met with President Xi Jinping of China in the Hague earlier this month. He has had something on the order of 17 or 18 meetings with Chinese Presidents and Prime Ministers since he took office. To the best of my knowledge, in every single meeting, President Obama made clear to his Chinese counterparts that the use of force, the use of coercion, the threat of force, and other means of intimidation are unacceptable as vehicles for advancing China's territorial claims. And the President has left the Chinese leadership in no doubt of our resolve.

Now, all that said, Senator, the fact is that there are diplomatic steps underway between China and the 10 ASEAN countries. There are also important discussions underway among the four ASEAN claimants themselves. We are confident that there are diplomatic paths to move forward on the disputes relating to the South China Sea, and we hope, although we do not take a position on the claims, that the net effect of the Philippine filing in the tribunal will be to encourage China to clarify its own claims in ways that are consistent with international law and remove the ambiguity that is destabilizing in our view.

Senator MURPHY. Thank you, Senator Rubio.

I think this is a really important line of questioning, and so I want to continue it with you, Mr. Secretary, and ask you one of Senator Rubio's questions in just a slightly different way. I am filling in for Senator Cardin here, but I normally chair the Subcommittee on European Affairs. So I have spent a good deal of the last 3 months in Ukraine and thinking about Ukraine. And so let me sort of make that connection again here.

There is a theory that suggests that if Russia gets away with this extraterritorial incursion into Crimea without consequences and without serious, crippling consequences, more likely to be on the economic side than on the military side, then that sends a message to other countries that may be considering similar extraterritorial action. It may send a message to elements within those countries that are trying to push for extraterritorial action that you can move on a disputed area or on another country without consequence. And the country that is most frequently brought up with respect to how this psychology may work is clearly China.

And so you have answered some of these questions, but I want to ask you directly about that suggestion that people have made, that if Russia effectively gets away with this without the United States and Europe delivering a substantial blow to Russian interests, do you agree that that sends a message to, maybe, not China at-large, but elements within China that may be contemplating the kind of action that Senator Rubio is talking about with respect to the Philippines or the Senkaku Islands or, God forbid, Taiwan that would give them additional reason to consider that kind of action given how the next several weeks and months play out in Crimea, Ukraine, and Russia?

Mr. RUSSEL. Well, thank you very much, Senator.

And of course, this is a question that we are looking at very carefully.

For my part, I approach it from the perspective of the Assistant Secretary for East Asia and the Pacific, and so I will stipulate at the outset that I am no expert on the Ukraine, Crimea, or Russia.

What I can report, Senator, is that the widespread perception in the region is one of, in the first instance, alarm at Russia's behavior and a deep interest and an intense attention on the response taken by the United States and the European Union acting in concert to rebuke the action, to condemn it, and to begin to impose consequences as a result.

I would characterize the response broadly within East Asia and particularly among the Southeast Asian countries where there are contentious territorial claims with China as one that has heightened their concern about the possibility of China increasingly threatening force or other forms of coercion to advance their territorial interests.

The net effect of this I think is to put more pressure on China to demonstrate that it remains committed to the peaceful resolution of problems. That is China's asserted position. And the tolerance in the region for steps by China that appear to presage a more muscular approach has gone down as their alarm over Russian action and annexation of Crimea has increased.

Senator MURPHY. I certainly understand what the reaction would be from China's neighbors. I guess my question is more putting on your China expert hat. What do we know about China's interpretation of the events that have taken place and how will they interpret the consequences that flow or do not flow to Russia moving forward? Or are they just not thinking about it in those terms?

Mr. RUSSEL. Thank you, Senator.

There is no doubt that China is thinking hard about the implications of Russia's annexation of Crimea and the international response. Of course, I would have to let the Chinese speak for themselves. It is difficult to guess what is in their heart of hearts.

But it is fair to say, Senator, that the extent of Chinese interdependence in economic terms with the United States and with its Asian neighbors is such that the prospect of the kind of incremental retaliatory steps that are gradually being imposed on Russia in terms of its banks, in terms of cronies, and in other areas should have a chilling effect on anyone in China who might contemplate the Crimea annexation as a model.

Senator MURPHY. Let me ask for your thoughts on the protests that have erupted in Taiwan with respect to this new economic agreement with China. There are reports out today that there is a new piece of legislation that would require the Cabinet to regularly engage with lawmakers and the public on future agreements with China. There are some initial reports that the protestors are suggesting that is not enough for them to end their occupation of government buildings.

I would appreciate an update on these protests from the State Department's perspective and maybe your take on what this says about the broader disagreement within Taiwan about the future course of relations with China.

Mr. RUSSEL. Well, thank you, Senator.

I mean, in the first instance, what it says is that Taiwan is a very robust democracy with a high tolerance for the expression of political views. Now, obviously, the United States very much hopes that the students and demonstrators will use that freedom responsibly, that they will behave in a civil and in a peaceful manner and certainly to avoid violence. But it is a reflection of a very open society in which debate is not only allowed but encouraged.

There are several issues at play. In the first instance, I would say that one issue under contention has to do with the mechanism and the procedure by which the cross-strait agreement in question, which is an agreement on trade and services, has been moved through the Legislative Yuan, through the Taiwan Parliament. That is something of a procedural issue.

There is also undoubtedly a substantive issue at play with mixed views within the Taiwan community, as you allude to, to the pace and the scope of agreements being reached between Taiwan and the PRC.

As a general matter, we very much welcome and applaud the extraordinary progress that has occurred in cross-strait relations under the Ma administration. And I should add that because it takes two to tango, that on the Beijing side, there is real credit due as well. The current Foreign Minister, Wang Yi, is a former head of the Taiwan Affairs Office. The current head of the Taiwan

Affairs Office in Beijing is a good friend of ours, former Vice Foreign Minister Zheng Zeguang. There is an extremely productive and deep dialogue underway across the strait which recently culminated in a visit by the Mainland Affairs Office Minister Wang to China, which was an extraordinary and historic milestone.

We do not, however, take a view on any particular agreement, and we believe strongly that the pace and the scope of movement in cross-strait discussions must be one that is in accord with the comfort level and the wishes of the people on both sides of the strait.

Senator MURPHY. Just to finish up, I really appreciate the way in which you framed the answer to that question. We are, obviously, watching these protests closely.

But it does demonstrate the initial point you made I think in the answer to Senator Rubio's first question about Taiwan's role with respect to our Rebalance to Asia and that it is a nation, maybe uniquely, that shares American values about the ability and the right of individuals to take part in government, protest their government. And as concerning as it may be to read about people occupying government buildings, at the same time it is a symbol of the important connection that we have with Taiwan regarding their ability to allow folks in that part of the world to speak for themselves.

Senator Rubio.

Senator RUBIO. I just have one final comment. Sorry I neglected to ask it. We were having a good conversation about the other issues.

Does the Obama administration remain committed to President Reagan's so-called Six Assurances to Taiwan? Is that still our position?

Mr. RUSSEL. Senator, thank you.

The underpinning of our policy is our One China Policy, the three United States-China joint communiques, and the Taiwan Relations Act. But the ''Six Assurances'' that you are referring to continue to play an important part as an element of our approach to Taiwan and the situation across the strait.

Senator RUBIO. All six of them remain the policy of the United States?

Mr. RUSSEL. What I would say, Senator, is that in the context of the agreements that I mentioned, what is known as the Six Assurances comprise an ongoing element of our approach to the Taiwan question.

Senator RUBIO. I guess my concern now is why cannot the answer be, yes, we remain committed to all six of them as elements of our foreign policy. Why are you unable to say that?

Mr. RUSSEL. Well, what I am trying to communicate, Senator, is that the underpinning of our approach to Taiwan is the One China Policy, the three communiques, and the Taiwan Relations Act. That having been said, what is known as the Six Assurances, which date back to the Reagan administration, as you say, are things that we take seriously and remain important elements as we formulate practical policies vis-a-vis——

Senator RUBIO. I am concerned about the answer because on a number of occasions, after meeting with the President, the Chinese have actually misrepresented. In fact, in one instance, the Chinese actually said that the United States policy toward Taiwan was evolving and changing. I understand you are not the decisionmaker about what our policy is, but I must say I am concerned that I am unable, from the administration, today to get a statement that the Six Assurances—all six—remain things we are firmly committed to as opposed to simply things that inform us or elements of our policy.

So I am not wrong then to leave here today and say that all Six Assurances remain elements of our policy, but they are no longer necessarily the cornerstone of our policy? The administration is not prepared to say that we remain committed to all six in their totality as understood by President Reagan when he enunciated them.

Mr. RUSSEL. I am not familiar with categorical statements of that nature in this or in recent administrations, and I think, Senator, that it is wisest to approach the challenges of Taiwan based on the agreements and the legislation that I have described, but mindful of the important elements that are captured in what you refer to as the Six Assurances including, for example, principles that we continue to abide by such as our unwillingness to engage in any sort of prior consultations or discussions with the Chinese regarding arms sales just as an example.

Senator RUBIO. All right. So let me just ask this. Does it continue to be the policy of the United States that we will maintain the capacity of the United States to resist any resort to force or other forms of coercion that would jeopardize the security or the social or economic system of the people on Taiwan? That remains our policy.

Mr. RUSSEL. Yes, it is.

Senator RUBIO. Thank you.

Senator CARDIN [presiding]. Secretary Russel, thank you very much. Again, we appreciate it and have a safe trip to Asia.

Mr. RUSSEL. Thank you very much, Mr. Chairman.

Senator CARDIN. We will now move to our second panel. We first have Mr. Abraham Denmark, vice president for Political and Security Affairs at the National Bureau of Asian Research. Mr. Denmark manages a team of experts and staff to bring objective, detailed analysis of geopolitical trends and challenges in Asia to the attention of Congress and other policymakers.

He is joined by Mr. Randy Schriver, president and chief executive officer of Project 2049 Institute, a nonprofit research organization dedicated to the study of security trendlines in Asia. He is also a founding partner in the Armitage International, LLC and a senior associate at the Center for Strategic and International Studies.

We welcome both of you and we will start with Mr. Denmark. And as I have indicated earlier, your full statements will be made part of the record, and you may proceed as you wish.

STATEMENT OF ABRAHAM M. DENMARK, VICE PRESIDENT FOR POLITICAL AND SECURITY AFFAIRS, THE NATIONAL BUREAU OF ASIAN RESEARCH, WASHINGTON, DC

Mr. DENMARK. Thank you, Mr. Chairman and members of the committee, for this opportunity to testify on the important issue of United States-Taiwan relations and the 35th anniversary of the

Taiwan Relations Act. And I should add as a resident of Silver Spring, it is especially a pleasure to be here today.

Senator CARDIN. That is why you are going first.

Mr. DENMARK. I appreciate it. [Laughter.]

I would also like to thank the subcommittee for holding a hearing on the TRA, the Senate's first in 15 years.

The National Bureau of Asian Research was founded 25 years ago in the memory of Senator Henry M. Jackson. Senator Jackson voted in favor of the Taiwan Relations Act in 1979, as did a bipartisan group of 85 Senators.

Since that vote, the TRA has been instrumental in preserving the stability in the Taiwan Strait and the rest of the region, fostering the growth of a robust democracy, enabling the emergence of the world's most innovative economies, and sustaining American presence and influence in the region. The TRA has also provided the strategic environment in which Taiwan and the PRC have been able to pursue stronger ties in recent years.

Relations between the United States and Taiwan are founded upon common interests in regional stability, shared commitments to the principles of economic and political liberalism, and a mutual respect for international law.

Taiwan was America's 12th-largest trading partner in 2013 with two-way trade surpassing $63 billion.

Taiwan is also a major security partner of the United States. Since 2009, the executive branch has notified Congress of over $12 billion in new defense articles and services for Taiwan, making Taiwan one of our top foreign military sales customers in Asia and one of the largest in the world.

In recent years, the TRA has also enabled Taiwan to emerge as an important player in regional geopolitics. Taiwan's international behavior exemplifies that of a responsible power from contributing to international disaster responses in Japan and the Philippines to demonstrating a constructive approach to addressing maritime disputes through its East China Sea Peace Initiative.

Today relations between Taipei and Beijing are quite positive. Since 2008, Taiwan and the PRC have reduced cross-strait tensions and focused on building economic and cultural ties. The results have been quite extraordinary. In 2013, for example, cross-strait trade rose to $197 billion.

Still, despite the cross-strait rapprochement, all is not well in the cross-strait relationship. The PRC's investment in military capabilities positioned across from Taiwan has continued unabated, and Beijing has refused to renounce the use of force. The PLA has amassed a force of more than 1,100 ballistic missiles along the Taiwan Strait as part of a layered, multidimensional military capability that remains primarily focused on Taiwan-related contingencies.

At the same time, Taiwan's investment in its own military capabilities has been stagnant. Taiwan's official defense budget for 2013 was $10.5 billion, while in the same year the PRC spent more 10 times that of $112 billion. The result has been an increasingly unbalanced cross-strait military dynamic. To address this imbalance, Taiwan's military has begun to pursue innovative asymmetric strategies to deter the PRC.

The United States and Taiwan should continue to work closely with one another to enhance Taiwan's ability to defend itself. Moreover, policy coordination on political and military issues should also be an important part of the bilateral relationship. Taiwan could potentially play a significant role in shaping the security environments of both the East and South China Seas.

Further, progress should be made in formalizing a bilateral investment agreement with the United States and bringing Taiwan into the Trans-Pacific Partnership. This would encourage Taipei to make significant progress in the liberalization of its economy while also diversifying Taiwan's economic relationships and diluting the PRC's ability to coerce Taiwan in a time of crisis.

The future of the cross-strait dynamic is uncertain. How Beijing's leaders may react to a DPP electoral victory and will ultimately calculate the success of its current engagement strategy with Taiwan and how it will weigh that strategy against alternatives is unclear.

To conclude, the Taiwan Relations Act has for 35 years been the foundation for a robust relationship between Washington and Taipei that has grown to include all elements of national power. Preserving and expanding the benefits of the TRA will be a necessary element in America's efforts to sustain its power and influence in the Asia-Pacific, to maintain regional stability, and to promote its interests and valued throughout the region.

Thank you again for inviting me today.

[The prepared statement of Mr. Denmark follows:]

PREPARED STATEMENT OF ABRAHAM M. DENMARK

INTRODUCTION

Mr. Chairman and other members of the subcommittee, thank you for the opportunity to testify on the important issue of U.S.-Taiwan relations and the 35th anniversary of the Taiwan Relations Act (TRA). I would like to thank you, Mr. Chairman, for your leadership and strong support for U.S.-Taiwan relations, as well as robust U.S. economic and strategic engagement in the Asia-Pacific as we rebalance toward the region. As a resident of Silver Spring, it is a special privilege to be here with you today. I would also like to thank the subcommittee for holding a hearing on the TRA—the Senate's first in 15 years.

My institution, The National Bureau of Asian Research, was founded 25 years ago in the memory of Senator Henry M. Jackson. Senator Jackson voted in favor of the Taiwan Relations Act in 1979, as did a bipartisan group of 85 Senators that included our current Vice President, Bill Bradley, Bob Dole, Barry Goldwater, Jessie Helms, Daniel Inouye, Ted Kennedy, and Sam Nunn.

The TRA has enjoyed robust bipartisan support ever since, through six administrations. This support naturally flows from the TRA's strategic significance to American interests and its value as the foundation for U.S. relations with Taiwan—one of our nation's key strategic partners in the Asia-Pacific.

STRATEGIC IMPORTANCE OF THE TRA

The Taiwan Relations Act was one of the most consequential foreign policy acts of Congress during the cold war. It established six features of American foreign and national security policy that remain highly relevant today, asserting the following U.S. policies:

1. To preserve and promote extensive, close, and friendly commercial, cultural, and other relations between the people of the United States and the people on Taiwan, as well as the people on the China mainland and all other peoples of the Western Pacific area;

2. To declare that peace and stability in the area are in the political, security, and economic interests of the United States, and are matters of international concern;

3. To make clear that the United States decision to establish diplomatic relations with the People's Republic of China [PRC] rests upon the expectation that the future of Taiwan will be determined by peaceful means;

4. To consider any effort to determine the future of Taiwan by other than peaceful means, including by boycotts or embargoes, a threat to the peace and security of the Western Pacific area and of grave concern to the United States;

5. To provide Taiwan with arms of a defensive character; and

6. To maintain the capacity of the United States to resist any resort to force or other forms of coercion that would jeopardize the security, or the social or economic system, of the people on Taiwan.

Combined with the three U.S.-PRC Joint Communiques and the "Six Assurances," the TRA constitutes the bipartisan foundation for our "one China" policy. America's approach to Taiwan and the PRC has proven to be remarkably consistent. We insist that cross-strait differences be resolved peacefully and according to the wishes of the people on both sides of the strait. We do not support Taiwan independence and are opposed to unilateral attempts by either side to change the status quo. We welcome efforts on both sides to engage in a dialogue that reduces tensions and increases contacts across the strait. And we are committed to preserving peace and stability in the Taiwan Strait. As part of our commitments under the TRA, we continue to provide Taiwan with defensive military systems based on its needs and, following our longstanding policy, make decisions about arms sales without advance consultation with the PRC.

It is important to note that, as much as it may try, China cannot "reinterpret" U.S. policies toward Taiwan. As you may recall, after a meeting in the Pentagon between Secretary of Defense Chuck Hagel and Chinese Minister of Defense General Chang Wanquan in 2013 a Chinese military spokesman stated that the United States had agreed to establish a joint task force on the issue of arms sales. More recently, China's Foreign Ministry misrepresented discussions between President Obama and President Xi to suggest the U.S. policy toward Taiwan had changed. In both cases, U.S. officials clarified that U.S. policies regarding Taiwan had not changed.

These policies have enabled Taiwan to prosper in every sense of the word. The TRA has been instrumental in preserving stability in the Taiwan Strait (and, as a result, the region more broadly), fostering the growth of a robust democracy as well as one of the world's most vibrant cultures and innovative economies, and preserving American presence and influence in the region. The TRA has also provided the strategic environment in which Taiwan and the PRC have been able to nurture stronger political and economic ties in recent years.

While over the past 35 years the relationship between Taiwan and the United States has evolved and deepened, and cross-strait dynamics have changed dramatically, the continued relevance and importance of the TRA is a testament to the wisdom and foresight of those who wrote and approved it in 1979.

CURRENT STATUS OF U.S.–TAIWAN RELATIONS

While some in 1979 worried that the TRA represented the end of U.S.-Taiwan relations, the reality has been the opposite. Indeed, since 1979, U.S.-Taiwan relations have flourished. As the TRA makes abundantly clear, the United States has an abiding interest in maintaining peace and stability across the Taiwan Strait, values robust engagement with Taiwan, and sees a Taiwan that is able to defend itself as firmly within American interests.

Relations between the United States and Taiwan are founded upon common interests in regional stability, shared commitments to the principles of economic and political liberalism, and a mutual support for international law. Taiwan's open politics and its exuberant democracy are remarkable, and are regularly put on display through open elections and the exercise of an independent judiciary and media. Most recently, popular protests in Taiwan against a proposed services agreement with the PRC have served both as a reminder of the importance of free speech and peaceful assembly, as well as the vital need for the rule of law.

Contacts between the U.S. Government and the governing authorities on Taiwan are robust, as senior-level officials from both sides meet regularly. Taiwan was America's 12th-largest trading partner in 2013, with two-way trade surpassing $63 billion. In October 2013, Taiwan sent one of the largest delegations to the SelectUSA summit hosted by the Department of Commerce. In November, Taiwan's former Vice President, Vincent Siew, led an impressive delegation of Taiwan CEOs to the United States, announcing over $2 billion of new or ongoing investments in the United States. The economic relationship hit a major milestone in March 2013 when talks under our Trade and Investment Framework Agreement (TIFA) were restarted after a 6-year hiatus. While pork and beef remain difficult issues, our bilateral economic relationship encompasses a far broader set of industries and services.

Taiwan is also a major security cooperation partner for the United States. Since 2009, the executive branch has notified Congress of over $12 billion in new defense articles and services for Taiwan—making Taiwan our top foreign military sales customer in Asia and one of the largest worldwide. In particular, the United States has worked with Taiwan to enhance its ability to conduct humanitarian assistance and disaster relief (HA/DR) operations, which has recently been included as a core mission of Taiwan's Armed Forces. Taiwan has attended the MAHANI PAHILI exercise in Hawaii for the last 5 years, and the Hawaii National Guard is expanding its HA/DR relationship with Taiwan. Since 1997, the U.S. Air Force has also trained Taiwan's F–16 fighter pilots at Luke Air Force Base in Arizona.

The U.S. policy to rebalance toward the Asia-Pacific has been significantly beneficial to Taiwan's sense of security and confidence. This policy has reaffirmed America's commitment to sustain its influence and power in the region, and has reassured its allies and partners in the Asia-Pacific of America's continued presence and engagement. Overall, U.S. policy objectives for Taiwan—sustaining its ability to defend itself, deepening its economic and political engagement with the global economy, and expanding its diplomatic space—are fully compatible with Taiwan's own interests.

In recent years, the TRA has also enabled Taiwan to emerge as an important player in regional geopolitics. With its successful transition to a democratic form of government and its embrace of economic liberalism as a stable path for sustainable development, Taiwan has become a model for the entire region. Moreover, its international behavior exemplifies that of a responsible stakeholder—from contributing to international disaster responses in Japan and the Philippines to demonstrating a responsible approach to addressing maritime disputes through its East China Sea Peace Initiative. This initiative has not only demonstrated a roadmap for peaceful engagement, it has also enabled Taiwan to responsibly manage maritime incidents with Japan and the Philippines.

CURRENT STATE OF CROSS–STRAIT RELATIONS

Today, relations between Taipei and Beijing are generally very positive. Due to the policy decisions of the leadership on both sides, Taiwan and the PRC have since 2008 decided to reduce cross-strait tensions and focus on building economic and cultural ties. They were able to pursue such a rapprochement due to their mutual acceptance of the ''1992 Consensus,'' in which both sides recognized that there is only one China but agreed to differ on its definition. The results have been extraordinary—almost 3 million mainland Chinese visited Taiwan in 2013, up from just 300,000 in 2008. Cross-strait trade has risen by more than 50 percent since 2008, to $197 billion in 2013. Most recently, in February 2014, the heads of Taiwan's Mainland Affairs Council and China's Taiwan Affairs Office met for talks, representing the first formal meeting between ministers in their government capacities since the end of the Chinese Civil War in 1949.

Still, despite this rosy picture, all is not well in the cross-strait relationship. Beijing initially approved of this approach with the expectation that improving cross-strait economic and cultural ties would gradually pull Taiwan more closely into the PRC's orbit, thus enabling eventual unification. Yet trends have so far not born this out—according to polling in December 2013 by Taiwan's Mainland Affairs Council, 84.6 percent of the Taiwan people support the status quo for either the short or long term, and 51.9 percent see Beijing as hostile toward the Taiwan governing authorities. Political support for unification, therefore, remains minimal amongst Taiwan's population.

Moreover, despite significant warming in relations between Taipei and Beijing, the PRC's investment in military capabilities positioned across from Taiwan has continued unabated, and the People's Liberation Army (PLA) has experienced several years of double-digit annual growth in its budget. Beijing continues to refuse to renounce the use of force to compel unification, and has amassed a force of more than 1,100 ballistic missiles across the Taiwan Strait as part of a layered, multidimensional military capability that remains primarily focused on Taiwan-related contingencies.

Despite the PRC's continued robust investments in the PLA, Taiwan's investment in its own military capabilities has been stagnant for several years. Taiwan's official defense budget for 2013 was $10.5 billion, a decrease from the previous year. Taiwan spends 2.1 percent of its GDP on defense—far lower than historic levels and even lower than the 3 percent pledged by President Ma. Further force reductions

23

are on the horizon, as the Ministry of National Defense has announced its goal to reduce total forces from 215,000 to between 170,000 and 190,000 during the period from 2015 through 2019.

These trends have led to an increasingly unbalanced cross-strait military dynamic. While Taiwan's defense budget in 2013 was $10.5 billion, the PRC (according to the International Institute for Strategic Studies) spent 10 times more that year—$112 billion. By way of acknowledging that direct competition with the PLA is unfeasible, Taiwan's military has begun to pursue innovative, asymmetric strategies to deter a possible Chinese effort to invade, coerce, or attack Taiwan.

STRENGTHENING U.S.–TAIWAN RELATIONS

The Taiwan Relations Act should, along with the three Joint Communiques and the Six Assurances, continue to serve as the foundation for future engagement, cooperation, and coordination between the United States and Taiwan in the economic, political, and security spheres. Such interaction will necessarily be based on the shared interests on both sides to more deeply imbed Taiwan into the global economy, to build its international space, and to enhance Taiwan's ability to defend itself.

To more deeply imbed Taiwan into the global economy, progress should be made in formalizing a bilateral investment agreement with the United States and making progress toward bringing Taiwan into the Trans-Pacific Partnership (TPP). While participation in TPP would require the approval of all members, including the United States, such a move would encourage Taipei to make significant progress in the liberalization of its economy—a process that, while painful in the short-term, would have tremendous benefits for Taiwan over the medium and long term. Joining the TPP will not only help Taiwan further integrate itself into the regional economy, it will also help keep Taiwan's economy globally diversified and competitive. While this is a natural economic imperative, it is also a strategic requirement—diversification will dilute the PRC's ability to economically coerce Taiwan in a time of crisis.

International space is also an important issue for future U.S.-Taiwan cooperation. As described by Bonnie Glaser of the Center for Strategic and International Studies, several opportunities exist for Taiwan to expand their meaningful participation in organizations focused on civil aviation, climate change, promoting regional stability and prosperity, and telecommunications. While energy for this expanded profile will need to come from Taipei, Beijing can also play an important role in enabling greater space for Taiwan. For the United States, progress on this issue will mean working with both Taipei and Beijing—as well as other members of key institutions—to identify more opportunities for Taiwan to play a constructive role in organizations where issues of sovereignty do not apply.

On security issues, the United States and Taiwan should continue to work closely with one another to enhance Taiwan's ability to defend itself. Taiwan's recent decision to pursue an indigenous submarine capability is a positive development, and American strategists and naval experts should work closely with their counterparts in Taiwan to identify the capabilities necessary to enhance Taiwan's self-defense. Additionally, both sides must recognize that friendship occasionally requires the telling of hard truths. In this case, Washington should be clear with Taipei that Taiwan's flat defense budget is a persistent problem. The budget issue is particularly flummoxing in that both President Ma and the opposition Democratic People's Party (DPP) have publicly endorsed a defense budget at 3 percent of GDP. If there exists broad political support for such a budget level, why has spending continued to fall short of this benchmark in the face of a rapidly intensifying military challenge from the mainland? Addressing this issue should be a top priority for the U.S. and Taiwan defense establishments.

While issues of arms sales and enhanced planning will continue to be important in U.S.-Taiwan security relations, policy coordination on political-military issues should also be an important part of the bilateral relationship. Taiwan can potentially play a significant role in shaping the security environments of both the East and South China Seas. Beyond setting an example as a responsible regional stakeholder, Taiwan can help clarify the PRC's ambiguous claims in the South China Sea. As proposed by Jeffrey Bader, the former senior director for East Asian affairs on the National Security Council, Taiwan should clarify whether its claims in the South China Sea are consistent with international law.

Finally, continued cooperation on defense investments and changes to military planning should remain at the center of U.S.-Taiwan military relations. Both sides have a profound interest in enhancing Taiwan's ability to defend itself, and this is a realizable goal if both Washington and Taipei remain committed to pursuing

24

asymmetric and innovative military strategies and translating words on a page into real-world capabilities.

ASSESSING FUTURE CROSS–STRAIT DYNAMICS

As with any democracy, political power in Taiwan will eventually change hands as the result of democratic processes. As former Assistant Secretary of State for East Asia and the Pacific Kurt Campbell stated in 2011, no single party or leader on Taiwan has a monopoly on effective management of cross-strait relations. The United States should not take sides in this election and commit to working closely with whomever should win future free and fair elections in Taiwan. Yet we do have interests in Taiwan and in the cross-strait dynamic, and we should make those interests known.

Given that Taiwan's next Presidential election will be held in 2016, any prediction about the outcome of that election will be far from reliable. Yet the possibility that the DPP may regain power in Taiwan is a possibility that requires some consideration. There are lingering questions, in Beijing and elsewhere, about the DPP's ability to effectively and reliably manage cross-strait relations if and when it regains political power in Taipei.

The DPP's future direction remains unclear. DPP officials have recently sought to adjust the Party's approach to cross-strait relations, and this process is still ongoing. While the United States should refrain from inserting itself into Taiwan's electoral process and should continue to encourage and congratulate Taiwan on its democratic system of governance, the United States does have an interest in seeing that cross-strait stability and communication are maintained. This need not be the 1992 Consensus, but rather any formulation upon which Beijing and Taipei can continue their peaceful engagement.

China's reaction to a DPP election is also an issue deserving some consideration. There were several reports of attempts by China to influence past elections, though Beijing has certainly learned the lessons of 1996 that attempts at intimidation can backfire. My sense is that China will look to sustain cross-strait engagement and communication in if the DPP comes back to power, provided that a mutually acceptable concept for engagement can be found. Yet how Beijing's leaders will ultimately calculate the success of its current engagement strategy, and how it will weigh that strategy against alternatives, is very unclear.

While relations between Taiwan and the PRC may have improved since 2008, the recent protests in Taipei—as well as the largely symbolic nature of the first round of direct meetings—signal the domestic political limits on the potential for unification and the speed at which progress may occur. Since the cross-strait rapprochement has been based on pursuing easier issues (economic and cultural engagement) before difficult issues (politics and Taiwan's official status), the pace of engagement between the two sides may be plateauing.

While Xi Jinping has publicly stated that China supports Taiwan's ''social system and lifestyle,'' he has also stated that ''the longstanding political division between the two sides will have to be eventually resolved step-by-step as it should not be passed on generation after generation.'' Beijing's assessment of progress toward their goal of unification and Taiwan's continued structural unwillingness to change its de facto status will fundamentally define cross-strait dynamics over the long term.

CONCLUSION

For 35 years, the Taiwan Relations Act has been the foundation for a robust, if unofficial, relationship between Washington and Taipei that has grown to include all elements of national power. The human, economic, political, and strategic benefits of the TRA have been tremendous. Preserving and expanding the benefits of the TRA will depend on skilled statecraft from both sides and will be a necessary element in America's efforts to sustain its power and influence in the Asia-Pacific and to promote economic and political liberalism throughout the region.

Senator CARDIN. Thank you.
Mr. Schriver.

STATEMENT OF RANDALL G. SCHRIVER, PRESIDENT AND CHIEF EXECUTIVE OFFICER, PROJECT 2049 INSTITUTE, ARLINGTON, VA

Mr. SCHRIVER. Thank you very much, Mr. Chairman, for this opportunity and thank you for seating me with a colleague who I admire and respect a great deal, Mr. Denmark.

In the interest of time, I would just like to draw from my statement and just make a few observations on cross-strait relations, the United States-Taiwan relationship, and maybe some recommendations for going forward.

As I think both Secretary Russel and Mr. Denmark stated, the cross-strait relationship has enjoyed a lot of positive developments in recent years, and I believe President Ma deserves enormous credit for that, the ECFA agreement, the 21 agreements that have been achieved between the two sides.

But there are some concerning trends, and I would just make note of four trends. And one has already been addressed I think quite eloquently and that is the security environment. The military buildup opposite Taiwan continues apace. There has been no move to reduce the threat posture. In fact, it has continued to build despite the political improvements and the economic progress the two sides have made.

I think we are also concerned about Taiwan's need for international space and the continuing pressure from Beijing on other countries and on international organizations to prevent Taiwan from enjoying greater participation in international organizations and the international community.

Number three, I think we should also be concerned about these demonstrations, but more broadly what it says about the public and their views of the cross-strait relationship right now. Having just been in Taiwan last week, former Deputy Secretary Armitage and I took a group to Taiwan and had a chance to wander through some of these areas. And what is really at the core of the protest, I think, is very deep-seated anxiety about the future of the cross-strait relationship and what that might mean for Taiwan's status. So, yes, the proximate cause is this cross-strait service trade agreement but I think there is a very deep-seated anxiety, if not neuralgia, about where things are going, and that could put a brake a bit on future cross-strait progress and that is certainly something to be mindful of.

Then lastly, I think we need to look ahead of the coming 2016 election and look at China's behavior in the past. As Taiwan has held national elections, they in the past have conducted provocative missile exercises. They have made intimidating gestures and speeches to the public in Taiwan. And I think we should expect, particularly with where the polls are today, that China will try to put its thumb on the scales and influence the outcome of that election. And I think it is in our interest to do what we can to ensure that Taiwan has the ability to make decisions about its future by itself free of coercion to the extent possible.

Now, I think each of these trends that I mentioned suggest a role for the United States to support Taiwan and address Taiwan's needs. And I think they fall into several categories.

I think in the security area, we should be moving forward with some of the major weapons systems. I would cite submarines, a program that—I was part of the decisionmaking in 2001 in the Bush administration when we said that Taiwan needed these platforms and committed the United States to helping Taiwan acquire the platforms. But yet, here we are 13-plus years later and there is no program to speak of. And I think the requirement has only gotten more strong given China's submarine development and other military modernization efforts.

I think the United States should make a Cabinet-level visit to Taiwan. The Clinton administration sent three Cabinet Secretaries to Taiwan in 8 years. This administration has sent zero, like the administration just before it, the Bush administration.

I think the United States should be more positive and more open about Taiwan's interest in TPP. We should be talking about a roadmap and the ability of Taiwan to join that organization, not just welcome their interest in it. I understand the TIFA process is being resumed this week, but we should articulate a stronger interest in Taiwan joining that organization and provide a clear roadmap for their participation down the line.

And then finally, on arm sales more generally—I mentioned the submarine program in particular. I think this country should be committed to Taiwan's defense in a way that we have regular congressional notifications. The previous witness from the administration's comments notwithstanding about all the support we have given to Taiwan's military, it has, in fact, been the longest period of gap in congressional notifications in the history of the relationship since the Taiwan Relations Act was passed, 2½-plus years since the last congressional notification. I think this should be remedied. Taiwan not only needs the military systems, they need that show of support from the United States.

Thank you, Mr. Chairman.

[The prepared statement of Mr. Schriver follows:]

PREPARED STATEMENT OF RANDALL G. SCHRIVER

Mr. Chairman and esteemed committee members, I would like to express my appreciation for the opportunity to appear before your committee to address the landmark legislation that has governed relations between the United States and Taiwan for the last 35 years.

Since its enactment in 1979, the Taiwan Relations Act (TRA) has been the foundation upon which the United States and Taiwan have maintained their dynamic and enduring ties. For over 35 years, the United States has played an important role in ensuring Taiwan's security while maintaining constructive relations with the People's Republic of China (PRC). Enabled by the TRA, continuity in U.S. policy has preserved American credibility within the Asia-Pacific region and enabled the island's nascent democracy to flourish. U.S. support for Taiwan has served as a visible symbol of U.S. commitment to peace and security in the Asia-Pacific region. Taiwan also has an important role to play in the comprehensive U.S. Rebalance to Asia that was announced in 2011.

U.S.-TAIWAN RELATIONS

Taiwan's continued success as a democracy, free market economy, and responsible regional and global actor is a core interest of the United States. The United States and Taiwan engage cooperatively over a wide range of economic, security, and diplomatic issues. Our strong trade relationship alone demonstrates just how important the U.S.-Taiwan relationship is for U.S. interests. Taiwan is the United States 12th-largest trading partner and 16th-largest export market for U.S. goods.

27

There are many recent developments in U.S.-Taiwan trade relations that are positive. The resumption of the U.S.-Taiwan Trade and Investment Framework Agreement (TIFA) discussions, after a prolonged hiatus, has the potential to revitalize our trade ties. Taiwan's efforts to join the Trans Pacific Partnership (TPP) can also be an opportunity for U.S.-Taiwan relations. As an export-oriented economy with the world's 21st-largest GDP, Taiwan's membership would significantly enhance the trade pact by further integrating Taiwan's economy with that of the United States and other partners in the region. The TPP is an integral part of the U.S. rebalance and we have an important stake in ensuring that Taiwan is a part of it. In addition, through a reinvigorated bilateral economic relationship with the United States, Taiwan may be able to engage counterparts across the Taiwan Strait with greater confidence.

There is also a growing web of people-to-people exchanges between the United States and Taiwan. Taiwan's designation for participation in the Visa Waiver Program (VWP) in 2012 led to a significant rise in visits between the two countries. Recent visits by three U.S. Deputy Assistant Secretaries to Taiwan was an encouraging and refreshing sign of U.S. commitment to Taiwan, especially considering the dry-spell of high-level U.S. visits to Taiwan. These diplomatic and economic ties are augmented by an increasingly robust U.S.-Taiwan military-to-military relationship. Forging and nurturing these relationships between our militaries is not only important for our ability to address common challenges, but also reinforcing the security commitments to Taiwan that the United States affirmed with passage of the TRA 35 years ago.

While the above-mentioned areas of U.S.-Taiwan relations are progressing well, more could be done. Despite closer cross-strait engagement, there is understandable consternation in Taipei and around the region regarding PRC military modernization and deployments opposite Taiwan, particularly in light of the PRC's refusal to renounce use of force against Taiwan to resolve differences. Forwarding of the Six Assurances under the Reagan administration to Taiwan in 1982 reinforced language contained in the TRA to provide Taiwan with arms according to its defensive needs. It also provided Taiwan with a guarantee that we would not hold prior consultations with the PRC regarding arms sales to Taiwan. This assurance should remain central to U.S. decisionmaking on security assistance to Taiwan. The prolonged absence of a congressional notification on Taiwan arms sales could be perceived as accommodating Chinese positions and potential reaction to a formal announcement, as the People's Liberation Army (PLA) continues to develop and deploy capabilities intended to coerce and/or facilitate use of force against Taiwan.

This administration needs bolder and more visible measures to fulfill U.S. obligations to Taiwan consistent with notification requirements under the Arms Export Control Act. The United States should avoid allowing interests in preserving positive atmospherics in the China relationship to come at the cost of relations with Taiwan and its legitimate defense needs.

Guided by the TRA and Six Assurances, Taiwan is not simply an "issue to manage" in U.S.-China relations. There are significant opportunity costs to treating Taiwan as a subordinate issue in U.S.-China ties rather than as legitimate government able and willing to help resolve a broad range of shared challenges faced by the international community. Opportunities for cooperating with Taiwan are significant in areas ranging from climate change, disaster response, to counterproliferation. In short, Taiwan and its people have intrinsic value to the United States and broader international community separate from the context of U.S.-China relations. Given the comprehensive goals of the U.S. rebalance policy, Taiwan should be seen as a potential partner across the full spectrum of activities that support the rebalance.

CROSS-STRAIT RELATIONS

Cross-Strait relations have enjoyed positive developments in recent years. Since entering office in 2008, President Ma Ying-jeou's administration has prioritized the improvement of cross-strait relations. Since then, the two sides have established direct commercial flights between Taiwan and China, promoted bilateral tourism, and signed an Economic Cooperative Framework Agreement (ECFA).

The most recent breakthrough in cross-strait ties occurred on February 11, 2014, when Taiwan and China held their first official government-to-government talks since 1949. The meeting was historically significant in its own right, particularly because PRC government representatives were willing to acknowledge the legitimacy of government counterparts from Taiwan and meet on the basis of equality. From Beijing's perspective, there may be a greater sense of urgency to pressure Taiwan into political talks as the next national election in 2016 draws closer.

Despite political and economic gains in cross-strait relations, security issues continue to be a contentious issue. Last November, Beijing's announced an Air Defense Identification Zone (ADIZ) in the East China Sea, which overlapped with those of Taiwan, Japan, and South Korea. Two months ago, in response, Taiwan conducted a rescue exercise in an area where ADIZs of Taiwan, Japan, and China overlap to challenge the legitimacy of China's ADIZ. These events were a prominent reminder of the continuing tensions that underlie cross-strait relations.

Moreover, recent protests in Taipei demonstrate limitations in public willingness to further deepen economic links across the Taiwan Strait. Irrespective of how the government and students resolve disagreements, what these protests reveal is a deep-seated anxiety and suspicion on Taiwan toward further integration with the mainland.

Taiwan's requirement for defense articles and services are driven by the nature of the challenge posed by the PLA's continued military buildup opposite Taiwan. Buoyed by a 12.2-percent increase in its defense budget from the previous year, the PLA continues to modernize and expand its military capabilities that could be arrayed against Taiwan. As the 2014 Quadrennial Defense Review notes, " the rapid pace and comprehensive scope of China's military modernization continues, combined with a relative lack of transparency and openness from China's leaders regarding both military capabilities and intentions."

Chinese military modernization has yielded significant increases in the PLA's power and advantages. According to analysts in the United States and Taiwan's Ministry of National Defense, China has more than 1,500 missiles targeted at Taiwan. The PLA has also developed and deployed other military capabilities in areas such as electronic warfare, counterspace, advanced fighter aircraft, and undersea warfare. Ultimately, Chinese military leaders seek capabilities that could support an attempt to physically occupy Taipei should a decision be made to do so.

The PLA is developing the capability to coerce political leaders on Taiwan to settle political differences on Beijing's terms, while simultaneously attempting to deter, delay, or deny U.S. intervention in case of conflict. Barring deeper and broader U.S. support, the dynamic balance of military forces across the Taiwan Strait may further embolden authorities in Beijing to consider use of force.

IMPACT OF THE 2016 ELECTION

Looking ahead to the 2016 Presidential elections in Taiwan, our overriding interest is to see Taiwan complete another free and fair election, and to then proceed with the subsequent peaceful transfer of power to a new President. The United States should remain neutral on the outcome and remain steadfast in our support for furthering shared democratic values between the United States and Taiwan. In doing so, we would improve upon the approach taken in the lead up to the 2012 election when the Obama administration took a number of steps that provoked suspicions of leaning to one side in the election. The United States should not choose sides in Taiwan's Presidential election. Rather, it should support processes that help Taiwan deepen the resiliency of its own democracy.

In past election cycles China has taken steps to try to put their "thumb on the scales" and impact the outcome of elections. In March 1996, China test-fired ballistic missiles in the waters surrounding Taiwan in a brazen attempt to intimidate voters. Four years later, then-Premier Zhu Rongji infamously used a finger wagging gesture on television threatening Taiwanese voters not to reelect then-President Chen Shuibian.

The PRC's methods of influencing public policies on Taiwan have become less overt but in many ways more sophisticated through the use of political warfare and other forms of coercive persuasion. We should remain vigilant against potential attempts by China to influence the democratic process on Taiwan as we approach the 2016 elections.

No matter which party governs the ROC after the March 2016 election, we have reason for high confidence that the next leader in Taipei will be capable of managing cross-strait relations. Both sides of the political spectrum on Taiwan have expanded contacts and dialogue with counterparts across the Taiwan Strait and both major parties are earnest in establishing policies that will preserve peace across the strait. We must hold the Chinese Communist Party to account for any actions not conducive to peace and stability after the election on Taiwan.

AREAS TO STRENGTHEN THE RELATIONSHIP

There are several where the United States should seek to strengthen ties with Taiwan. First, while we enjoy many benefits of strong U.S.-Taiwan relations, our default mode has been to keep them low-key and quiet. The United States should be open and transparent in its dealings with Taiwan, highlighting meetings as routine and normal interactions between two legitimate governments.

Second, the United States needs to raise the level of its interactions with Taiwan, including Cabinet-level visits to Taiwan. Such visits offer opportunities to be more vocal and demonstrate our pride in the strength of our bilateral ties.

Third, we should fulfill our longstanding commitment to assist Taiwan in its acquisition of diesel electric submarines. Options include forwarding the congressional notification for a design program through Foreign Military Sales channels that has been frozen for over 5 years; or alternatively, providing a clear roadmap to support U.S. defense industry assistance to a Taiwan indigenous submarine program. Either way, diesel electric submarines would provide Taiwan with a credible and survivable deterrent and therefore is in the best interests of the United States.

Fourth, and independent of the submarine issue, congressional notifications under the Arms Export Control Act serve as a visible demonstration of U.S. support under the TRA. Therefore, we should be intentional about forwarding congressional notifications on a routine and frequent basis in support of Taiwan's defense needs. Long gaps between congressional notifications create uncertainties in Taiwan, and may embolden leaders of the Chinese Communist Party to think they can cause coerced solutions to their differences with Taiwan.

Fifth, consistent with progress made in the TIFA process, the United States should endorse Taiwan's candidacy and create a roadmap for Taiwan's membership in the TPP.

Sixth, the United States should continue to support Taiwan's meaningful participation in international organizations such as International Civil Aviation Organization (ICAO). The United States should endorse Taiwan's full membership in ICAO, and should also seek creative approaches to increasing Taiwan's international profile in other areas.

Our commemoration of the 35th anniversary of the TRA is an excellent opportunity to reflect on current and past successes in U.S.-Taiwan relations. It is also an opportunity to chart a future path for our ties that is grounded in our legal obligations under the TRA to provide necessary support to allies and friends in a region where hard-power still matters. In midst of the U.S. rebalance to the Asia-Pacific, the U.S.-Taiwan relationship should be leveraged as a fundamental component of the U.S. rebalance and not a subissue in U.S.-China ties. Taiwan possesses intrinsic value as a flourishing democracy, an economic powerhouse, and most importantly, a longstanding security partner in East Asia.

I hope the Obama administration and friends in Congress will share this outlook. Thank you again Mr. Chairman for the opportunity to participate in your hearing today, and to offer these thoughts.

Senator CARDIN. Well, thank you both for your testimony.

The 35th anniversary of the formal agreement in regards to Taiwan—the Taiwan Relations Act—it is pretty specific as to our commitments in regards to Taiwan and our strong interest to make sure that peaceful relations exist in the region—and on the cross-strait issues, that Taiwan has the right of self-defense and our commitment to help them in self-defense. We have the three communiques and then we have President Reagan's comments on the assurances.

Are the fundamental agreements still sound today? This is 35 years later. There seems to be some hesitation in regards to some of the areas that we thought were pretty clear. You point out that high-level visits have not taken place as frequently if there are arms sale issues. Is there a need for any formal changes in your view on the underlying documents that underpin the relationship between the United States and Taiwan?

Mr. DENMARK. Thank you, Senator.

There have been several calls from the academic community here in D.C. and around the country for some sorts of changes to the Taiwan Relations Act, some saying it needs to be weakened, some saying that it needs to be strengthened. In my opinion, overall the Taiwan Relations Act is actually very sound in that it provides a robust foundation for engagement but also gives the administration enough room to maneuver to be flexible for existing and emerging contingencies. So overall, my assessment is that the Taiwan Relations Act in itself does not need to be revised, although the continuing discussion between the Congress and the administration, with this administration and previously, about the pace of arms sales, the size of arms sales, the pace of visits, the pace of contacts I think is very welcome in terms of pushing the relationship forward.

But if you look at how this administration has engaged Taiwan, I think it has actually been fairly robust. My friend, Randy, was very correct in the delay that we have seen, the lack of arms sales notifications that we have seen for the last 2 years, but I would say that a lot of that is because of the size of the significant notifications that came for a few years before that, leading to very significant notifications of arms sales and continued high-level meetings between political leadership on both sides, not a visit of a Cabinet Secretary to Taiwan yet, but continued regular senior-level meetings between the two sides.

I guess I do not see the visit of a Cabinet-level officer to Taiwan as being the litmus test for what constitutes a robust relationship. Rather, it is the regular meeting. The regular interaction of high-level officials across multiple elements of our two governments to me is the more important measure of our relationship, and to me the current administration has been fairly robust in its engagement.

Senator CARDIN. Let me ask you about United States-China relations as it relates to Taiwan. The United States has a somewhat complex relationship with China today. They are critically important in many of our discussions globally. How do you see what the United States does with Taiwan? This has been longstanding. Does it have impact on the bilateral relationship between China and the United States?

Mr. SCHRIVER. It certainly can, but my sense is many administrations, not just this one, try to overcorrect, overcompensate for the perceived reaction that we may get from China and place some limitations on what we would do with Taiwan. I think if you look at the actual record—we can stick with the subject of arms sales. I think if you actually look at the reaction, the fallout on the United States-China relationship has been consistent, quite predictable and quite manageable. So I think that should not really temper what we do with Taiwan.

And I would add on a Cabinet Secretary, I think that has been one of the points of reluctance is the fear that that particular Cabinet Secretary may not have continuing access to China should he or she visit Taiwan. But again, I think the past track record does not necessarily support that, and I think we should proceed. I obviously have a disagreement. I think it is important. We tell every other country it is important when our Cabinet Secretaries go. So I think this would be a very strong signal to Taiwan particularly in light of what they are facing right now in the cross-strait relationship.

Senator CARDIN. I think that is very important.

One of the things I think Senator Rubio and I will agree is that President Reagan was pretty definitive with his assurances. I personally think China respects that, a clear understanding of where the United States is, consistent with our historical commitments to the people of Taiwan. So I think a clear indication of where we stand helps not just the people of Taiwan but also helps in our bilateral relationship with China.

I want to ask one more question before turning it over to Senator Rubio, and that came up with Secretary Russel. One of the positive impacts of a better relationship between Taiwan and China is that Taiwan is a democracy. It is an open society. China is struggling on how to deal with more rights for its citizens. It has had an inconsistent path toward the type of democratic reforms that a country needs to do if it wants to be a major player on the world stage. And yet, the recent protests in Taiwan raises questions as to how effective Taiwan is in dealing with these issues.

How do you see these protests affecting the view in China as to the success of the Taiwan democracy?

Mr. SCHRIVER. Well, I think in this particular instance, it is probably a bit too soon to tell, but I think it is part of an overall picture that China is getting. They watch the elections. They watch the speeches of losing candidates and are amazed that people of wealth and privilege are willing to concede defeat and step away from power. They visit in greater numbers through tourism. And so they are seeing an awful lot, and I cannot help but to think that it is impacting them.

That said, what we see in China is I think a bit of a heavier hand on the Internet, on religious freedom, on human rights organizations. So I believe just sort of intuitively that the lessons are sinking in and are impacting people in China, but it has certainly yet to show up in how the authorities in Beijing are governing the PRC.

Senator CARDIN. I am going to turn the gavel over to Senator Rubio. As I indicated earlier, we have a markup going on in one of the committees I serve on. Senator Rubio, take as much time as you want.

Senator RUBIO [presiding]. Thank you.

And I too have to go to a meeting, but there are a couple important questions that I wanted to ask you and Senator Cardin just outlined this. I wanted to get back to this topic of the Six Assurances under the Reagan administration because I think to be clear and unequivocal with regard to that is critically important in terms of the message that we send and, quite frankly, the balance in the region.

I asked that question of Secretary Russel a moment ago. You were both in the audience and you heard his answer. And I wanted to get your impressions after hearing—I tried multiple different ways to get someone from the administration to tell me that the Six Assurances remain the cornerstone of our policy and that we still stand by those assurances. I do not think I got that, and I wanted your interpretation of the answer that we got with regard to that question.

Mr. SCHRIVER. I was surprised that it was not a more direct response and that it could not be made in the affirmative. Certainly when we were in Government, we would have said, absolutely yes, and did on many occasions. So I hope the administration has the opportunity to clarify that because I think the signal that it sends is a reassuring one if our friends in Taiwan know that they still apply in their totality as your question asked.

Senator RUBIO. Mr. Denmark, did you have a comment?

Mr. DENMARK. Thank you, Senator.

I think the Six Assurances, as you said, are incredibly important in our relationship. I certainly cannot speak for the administration. It is my sense that United States policy regarding Taiwan, including the Six Assurances, have not changed. There were some public comments from other administration officials a few weeks ago on this topic, specifically after the Chinese Foreign Ministry misreported interactions between President Obama and President Xi which stated explicitly that United States policy toward Taiwan had not changed. And I assume that that is still the guiding remarks from the administration.

Senator RUBIO. I would hope that that is the case. I again tried on multiple occasions to get a direct answer, a yes or no, yes, they remain part of our strategy. And it seems like they are elements of our strategy that might inform us according to the answer that I got. And I hope we can bring some clarity to it because I was surprised by the answer myself, and I did not think it was a hard question. I just wanted to get it in the record, and unfortunately, we did not get the answer we want, which I think actually is counterproductive.

In fact, I think that in China that answer that was given here today could potentially be misinterpreted as, in fact, an opening of some sort for a change in the United States posture toward Taiwan. I am very concerned about the answer that we got, and I hope that we can bring some clarity to it over the next few days. And I intend to ask that question as well in writing of the Secretary of State to get clear assurances that that remains a cornerstone of our policy.

I wanted to ask one more question. Mr. Denmark, this ties to your statement, although I would love to hear from both of you about it. You talked a little bit about the relations between Taipei and Beijing are generally very positive due to policy decisions of the leadership of both sides that, since 2008, decided to reduce the tensions and focus on building economic and cultural ties. And you say in your written statement that Beijing initially approved of this approach with the expectation that improving cross-strait economic and cultural ties would gradually pull Taiwan more closely to the PRC's orbit, thus enabling eventual unification.

Yet trends so far have not borne this out given, for example, even the events that are going on today with student protests regarding potential increased links with China.

Given that assessment, what impact do both of you think that now has on Chinese thinking? In essence, they have allowed this little opening to occur under the hopes that this would slowly but surely bring Taiwan closer to them until ultimately there would be a mutually agreed-to unification. Now they are seeing this sort of dynamic internally where people are saying we do not want to be closer to China. What impact could that have in your mind on how China approaches this relationship moving forward?

Mr. DENMARK. Thank you, Senator. It is a fascinating set of issues, a very difficult set of questions.

Overall, my sense is that Beijing remains committed to its approach in terms of engaging Taiwan, although with all due caveats of anybody's ability outside of Zhongnanhai in Beijing to read the thinking and feelings of Chinese senior leadership. So with that as a caveat, my sense is that they remain committed to engagement because they do see benefits—political, economic, and strategic benefits—for the engagement, but also the counterpart, the alternatives to that strategy remain very unclear in terms of if they would be more beneficial to China's overall strategy.

My sense, talking to scholars in China and from what I have read coming out of China, is that there is a lot of focus on the results of the election in 2016, that there is a lot of concern in China that if the DPP were to win power back, that Taiwan may revert back to the policies of Chen Shui-bian.

My sense is that the DPP is actually moving beyond that approach, that that would probably not happen again if the DPP were to win the next election. The DPP is actually going through a process of internally thinking about its own cross-strait policy, its own approach to these issues, and is working on a new formulation. And my sense is that Beijing, should the DPP win, would try to find some way to continue to work with them to continue this form of engagement.

As Randy pointed out earlier, I think it is very important that there have been reports of the mainland attempting to influence elections, and I suspect that this would probably continue because they see the importance of the election to Taiwan's behavior and how, post-2016, the mainland may calculate its options, may calculate the continued attractiveness of its engagement strategy I think is one too far for anybody to predict, especially outside of Zhongnanhai, but also the variables, the calculations are just far too complicated at this point to see really how Beijing may react to that scenario.

Mr. SCHRIVER. Thank you, Senator.

I think China's policies have not changed and probably will not for the foreseeable future, but with the trends in Taiwan, particularly the public polling about how people feel about their eventual status after the current status quo, one wonders does Beijing have unlimited patience. I suspect they do not because their ultimate objective appears to be getting further away. Their ultimate objective is clear. They want unification or what they call reunification. The polling suggests that goal is getting further away, which is why I think our support for Taiwan's security needs remain very relevant even in this era when there are improvements in the cross-strait political and economic relationship. If Beijing understands its policies are not bringing it closer to its ultimate objective, then the option of the use of force could become more attractive particularly if we are not doing our part in helping Taiwan with its defense needs.

Senator RUBIO. First of all, I appreciate both of you being here today and thank you for your testimony and thank you for your time.

That is exactly our concern, that any sort of weakening or questioning or equivocation on the part of the United States stance toward Taiwan, in fact invite miscalculation or recalculation on the part of the Chinese. And if people think that what is happening in Crimea is complicated, they have no idea what any sort of territorial dispute in this part of the world would look like. It would be incredibly destabilizing. It would have an immediate impact on the way Japan and South Korea and other nations portray themselves.

And I think the two nations right now who feel the most immediately threatened by the aggressiveness of the Chinese Government—one is the Philippines because they simply do not have the capability, and the other is Taiwan. I think that any sort of weakening or any sort of confusion about where the United States stands and our commitment to this relationship invite potential aggressiveness and aggression in a way that could end up finding us in a conflict that is much more complicated and in fact much more dangerous than even what we are seeing around the world today.

Again, I thank you both for being here and for your time and for your testimony.

The record for this hearing will remain open until the close of business Friday. Members and others will be allowed to submit stuff for the record or ask questions. And I would just ask for your cooperation that if you receive any questions between now and Friday, that you would answer them for the committee promptly so we can include it in our record.

And with that, the committee stands adjourned.

[Whereupon, at 11:22 a.m., the hearing was adjourned.]

ADDITIONAL MATERIAL SUBMITTED FOR THE RECORD

RESPONSES OF ASSISTANT SECRETARY DANIEL R. RUSSEL TO QUESTIONS SUBMITTED BY SENATOR MARCO RUBIO

Question. Is the administration committed to President Reagan's so-called "Six Assurances" to Taiwan?

Answer. The United States remains firmly committed to the U.S. one-China policy, the Three Joint Communiques, and our responsibilities under the Taiwan Relations Act. The so-called "Six Assurances" also are an integral part of our overall approach to Taiwan. Taken together, these commitments and assurances form the foundation of our relations with Taiwan.

The United States has long maintained that cross-strait differences are matters to be resolved peacefully, without the threat or use of force, and should be acceptable to the people on both sides of the Taiwan Strait. There is no change in our position. Our commitments and assurances to Taiwan are firm and long-standing.

Question. Do you expect a resumption of U.S. Cabinet-level visits to Taiwan this year? If so, which ones and when? If not, why?

Answer. U.S. Environmental Protection Agency (EPA) Administrator Gina McCarthy traveled to Taipei April 13–15, 2014, to highlight 20 years of environmental cooperation between the United States and the Taiwan authorities and promote environmental education. The EPA Administrator holds a Cabinet-rank position.

Question. As Taiwan is likely to retire some of its older fighter aircraft in the next 5 to 10 years, do you believe that sales of advanced aircraft and other weapon systems are an important, next step in this commitment?

Answer. The United States is firmly committed to the policy reflected in the Taiwan Relations Act enacted 35 years ago, which forms the basis of U.S. security cooperation with Taiwan. The TRA declares that it is U.S. policy to provide arms to Taiwan of a defensive character and that peace and stability in that area of the world are in the United States interest. The United States one-China policy, based on the Three Joint Communiques and the Taiwan Relations Act, has been consistent for the past 35 years, including six consecutive U.S. Presidencies.

We have a robust dialogue with the Taiwan authorities focused on military preparedness, threat perceptions and means to deter perceived threats.

The President and the Congress determine the nature and quantity of defense articles and services to sell to Taiwan-based solely upon their judgment of the needs of Taiwan. The volume of our arms sales to Taiwan is substantial. Consistent with our one-China policy, the Obama administration has notified Congress of its intent to sell Taiwan over $12 billion worth of new defense articles and services. Such sales support both our commitments to Taiwan and our interest in maintaining stability across the Taiwan Strait and in the region.

Signed contracts include an extensive retrofit and modernization of Taiwan's F-16 fleet, and the sale of Apache attack and Blackhawk transport helicopters, Patriot PAC-3 Air and Missile Defense Batteries, P-3C long range ocean surveil- lance and antisubmarine aircraft, Harpoon antiship missiles, Osprey-class coastal mine hunters, and a variety of other systems, training, upgrades, and advanced weapons and equipment.

We support Taiwan's efforts to develop innovative and asymmetric capabilities to deter coercion or intimidation, and we encourage Taiwan to increase its defense budget to a level commensurate with the security challenges it confronts. We do not comment on pending or potential arms sale requests.

Question. In 2001, The U.S. Government pledged to support Taiwan in its acquisition of diesel electric submarines. Today, it appears more and more likely that Taiwan will pursue a domestic submarine program with advice and support from foreign defense industry experts.
  - ♦ Would the administration support U.S. industry working with Taiwan on an indigenous program?
  - ♦ Is there any reason to think U.S. companies would be denied opportunities to support Taiwan's submarine program?

Answer. We do not comment on pending or potential arms sale requests.

The U.S. decision about diesel submarines is still under consideration. No decision has been made.

Question. Defense News recently reported that, despite the cancellation of the combat avionics programmed extension suite (CAPES), Taiwan will be able to progress with radar upgrades for its fleet of F-16s through savings in the contracting process. While this is good news for Taiwan in the short term, it is hard to believe that the long-terms costs for the radar and avionics won't spiral out of control without the additional 300 U.S. F-16's planned upgrades moving forward that would have kept supply chain and life-cycle costs low.

  - ♦ What options are we providing our partner to ensure that we are fulfilling our commitments under the Taiwan Relations Act?
  - ♦ Does the Department of Defense support allies and partners exploring competi- tions for these critical programs, to keep costs down?

Answer. The Taiwan Relations Act states that it is U.S. policy: "to consider any effort to determine the future of Taiwan by other than peaceful means, including by boycotts or embargoes, a threat to the peace and security of the Western Pacific area and of grave concern to the United States; to provide Taiwan with arms of a defensive character; and to maintain the capacity of the United States to resist any resort to force or other forms of coercion that would jeopardize the security, or the social or economic system, of the people on Taiwan."

U.S. Foreign Military Sales regulations state that programs for our foreign partners, to include Taiwan, are treated as if the program is for a U.S. Military Service. Therefore, all options are explored to keep costs down. However, U.S. law prohibits the United States from losing any money on such sales programs.

United States Air Force (USAF) funding for the CAPES program will continue through FY 2014. The USAF F-16 program office has determined that the lack of USAF participation beyond FY 2014 will not have a significant impact on the Taiwan program, and that any additional funding required and in commitments to this retrofit program can be covered in Taiwan's current Letter of Offer and Acceptance (LOA).

The CAPES cancellation is expected to have no impact to the operational capability of Taiwan's Retrofit Program. Taiwan's F-16 Retrofit Program continues to execute as planned in terms of performance, schedule and cost. While Taiwan will be solely responsible for funding the radar development for FY15 and beyond, no additional costs to Taiwan beyond the topline dollar figure in the LOA will be required.

Question. There have been suggestions that the easing of tensions between Taiwan and China has allowed China's People's Liberation Army (PLA) to concentrate on other contingencies such as the East China Sea and the South China Sea—and that increasingly a Taiwan scenario is less and less a driver for PLA modernization.

♦ Do you agree with this view?
♦ Is Taiwan still central to the PLA modernization goals?

Answer. We continue to carefully monitor China's military developments and encourage China to exhibit greater transparency with respect to its capabilities and intentions. In the absence of greater transparency, it is difficult to understand the motivations and goals of the People's Liberation Army (PLA), in particular, China's military leaders have not explained what scenarios are current within the PLA's contingency planning. We encourage China to use its military capabilities in a manner conducive to the maintenance of peace and stability in the Asia-Pacific region.

We urge China to continue its constructive dialogue with the authorities on Taiwan, which has led to significant improvements in the cross-strait relationship. We welcome the steps authorities on both sides of the Taiwan Strait have taken to reduce tensions and improve relations. However, China has never renounced the use of force against Taiwan and its military deployments across the strait from Taiwan continue to produce tension and uncertainty.

We will continue to encourage China to be transparent about its military spending and modernization. As part of that effort, we support the continued development of military-to-military relations as a key component of the U.S.-China bilateral relationship, characterized by sustained and substantive dialogue, a commitment to risk reduction, and practical, concrete cooperation in areas of mutual interest.

Question. What is the administration's view on inviting Taiwan to join the Trans-Pacific Partnership negotiations?

Answer. We welcome Taiwan's interest in the Trans-Pacific Partnership (TPP), and we note Taiwan's ongoing efforts to assess its readiness to take on the TPP's ambitious commitments. The TPP is open to regional economies that can demonstrate this readiness and gain consensus support of the current TPP members for them to join. Right now, the original 12 TPP members are focused on concluding the negotiations of the TPP agreement.

In the near term, consultations under the Trade and Investment Framework Agreement (TIFA) provide a substantive opportunity for Taiwan to resolve existing U.S. trade and investment concerns, demonstrate its preparations to take on new trade commitments, and set itself on a path of liberalization of its economic regime.

Question. What steps will the administration take to ensure that the United States does not interfere in the internal democratic process in Taiwan in the runup to the 2016 Presidential elections, especially given the unfortunate leak to the Financial Times in 2012 that implied that the United States favored one Presidential candidate over the other?

Answer. Free and fair elections are essential to a healthy democracy. As in the past, we will refrain from any action likely to be perceived as showing favoritism among candidates for elected office on Taiwan. Respect for democracy and the practice of democratic elections arc among the treasured values that the people of the United States share with the people on Taiwan. Through American Institute in Taiwan (AIT) offices in Taipei, Kaohsiung, and Washington, we will reach out to all political parties in Taiwan to learn about candidates and the parties' and candidates' prospective policies, conducting such outreach in a manner consistent with the unofficial nature of our relations with the authorities and people on Taiwan.

————

RESPONSE OF ASSISTANT SECRETARY DANIEL R. RUSSEL TO QUESTION
SUBMITTED BY SENATOR JOHN BARRASSO

Question. During your confirmation hearing, I asked you to commit to advocating for the elimination of trade barriers for soda ash and other important U.S. industries in the international marketplace.

In response to my question, you explained, "If confirmed as Assistant Secretary, I will prioritize the East Asian and Pacific (EAP) Bureau's promotion of U.S. exports and the facilitation of U.S industries' participation in international markets."

In addition, you indicated that you were aware that some countries have taken actions against the importation of soda ash.

You responded, "I will also advocate strongly for U.S. firms and industries, encouraging our trading partners' adherence to their international trade obligations in providing nondiscriminatory market access for our exporters, including those in the soda ash industry.''

♦ (1) How have you strongly advocated for market access for U.S. exporters in the soda ash industry?

♦ (2) What specific actions have you taken to address Taiwan's 3.5 percent tariff on imported soda ash?

♦ (3) What specific actions have you taken to address China's reinstituted 9 percent value added tax (VAT) rebate for soda ash exporters?

♦ (4) What specific actions have you taken to address Japan's 3.3 percent tariff on natural soda ash imports?

Answer. The State Department's Bureau of East Asian and Pacific Affairs is working closely with the office of the United States Trade Representative (USTR) to help secure important new market opportunities, including soda ash sales, for U.S. exporters.

On Taiwan, the United States will continue to engage with Taiwan authorities to support efforts by U.S. exporters and Taiwan importers to petition Taiwan to reduce its soda ash duties, as appropriate.

Regarding China, we have used bilateral fora—such as the Joint Commission on Commerce and Trade and the Strategic and Economic Dialogue—to encourage China to open its markets and reduce distorting practices such as tariffs, advantageous provisions for its state-owned enterprises, direct export subsidies, and VAT reimbursements for exporters such as those applied to soda ash exported from China.

In terms of Japan, the Trans-Pacific Partnership (TPP) will be a valuable tool in reducing Japan's tariffs on imports such as soda ash. Japan's participation in the TPP negotiations provides an important opportunity for many U.S. exporters—including U.S. soda ash exporters—to expand their access to the Japanese market.

www.ingramcontent.com/pod-product-compliance
Lightning Source LLC
Chambersburg PA
CBHW052021280526
45793CB00005B/1078